MW00588377

Buddhism is a rapidly rising religion in the West, but few Westerners know Buddhism from the inside. Having grown up with Buddhism and Christianity, Steve Cioccolanti highlights the similarities and builds bridges of understanding between the two major religions.

His account is studded with stories, parables, and illuminating observations. This book is remarkably easy to read, and Steve is an engaging and original guide. Discover Buddhism the way it's actually lived, not the way it's been presented in textbooks or by Hollywood. Now you can learn the 2 most popular religions in 1 book!

A groundbreaking book... Steve has an unusual insight into the Buddhist mind. I would use it for our Bible College students.

DR. WAYNE CORDEIRO, USA
Pastor of New Hope Christian Fellowship,
a 10,000+ member church in Hawaii.

From Buddha to Jesus is a clear exposition of both Buddha's search for truth and the foundations of Buddhist culture. It then gives an account of how the Good News of Jesus can fulfill Buddhist law, and deliver people from the drive of endless perfectionism. A totally thought-provoking work!

ROD PLUMMER, JAPAN
Senior Pastor of Jesus Lifehouse Tokyo

Steve's book 'From Buddha to Jesus' is the best tool that I have found to find a common platform with Buddhists. Although the book is primarily focused on Thai Buddhism, the principles in the book can be used with Buddhists in Japan and with Buddhists in other countries. I highly recommend it!

REV. DANIEL KIKAWA, USA
President of Aloha Ke Akua Ministries,
Pastor of Hilo Missionary Church, Author and producer of
the award-winning films of *God's Fingerprints in Japan 1 & 2*

One of the books that I really read from cover to cover. I bought 10 copies and distributed them to my friends. I was once a Buddhist and this book really opened up my eyes. It is a must-read for all Buddhists, Eastern religion followers or even Christians who are looking for a way to reach out to these groups of people. Steve Cioccolanti was able to put things in the right manner and has written in a balanced and non-offensive way. This book rocks!

DANIEL HENDRATA, INDONESIA
TV Host, Chairman & Co-Founder of Anugrah Ministries

I have been a missionary in Thailand for 40 years. I read your book and was very impressed. I wish I would have had it sooner.

DOROTHY H., THAILAND

I am a Malaysian Chinese... I was a Buddhist. I came across your explanation about Buddhism and found that it was so true!

SULEE, MALAYSIA

Steve's gentle way of sharing his insight suits the [Asian] audience very well... He has also broken some invalid preconceived ideas that Buddhists are closed to the Gospel.

CHING WAH, SINGAPORE
Former Pastor of the Anglican Church in Thailand

My husband and I have been reading it and although I am a second-generation missionary in Thailand (my dad arrived in 1946!) your book has brought new insight and clarified many things and is helping me/us immensely in relating to the Buddhists. So, Thank YOU and Thank GOD!

MARIANNA & ERIK, THAILAND
Missionaries

This book gave me confidence that I had a strategy! Because we can start from a place of commonality, instead of a place of 'I'm right, you're wrong'. This teaching releases people!

TIM P., THAILAND

Your book is one of my treasured collection and I've been reading it again and again. I love it so much. It helps me to understand Buddha and Buddhism and draw bridges between the two faiths. Keep up the good work and God bless!

MISH N., MALAYSIA

Anyone who comes in contact with Eastern religions should read Steve's book.

COL STRINGER, AUSTRALIA
President of ICFM Australia

Truly enlightening and informative... A useful tool to reach not only Buddhists but many others confused by the plethora of religions.

TOM INGLIS, AUSTALIA
Founder of Psalmody

A well-written book with a clear and bold testimony.

CANON JAMES WONG, SINGAPORE
Anglican Churches Singapore

# FROM BUDDHA TO JESUS

## AN INSIDER'S VIEW OF BUDDHISM

### STEVE CIOCCOLANTI

FROM BUDDHA TO JESUS: AN INSIDER'S VIEW OF BUDDHISM & CHRISTIANITY by Steve Cioccolanti

Published by Discover Media

Cover design by Selena Sok & Cathy Wong

selena@discover.org.au & cathy@discover.org.au

*This book or parts thereof may not be reproduced in any form, stored in a retrieval system or transmitted in any form by any means – electronic, mechanical, photocopy, recording or otherwise – without prior written permission of the publisher.*

Unless otherwise noted, all Scriptures quoted are from the New King James Version of the Bible. Copyright © 1979, 1980, 1982 by Thomas Nelson Inc. Used by permission.

Scripture quotation marked RSV is from the Revised Standard Version of the Bible. Copyright © 1952 by The Division of Christian Education, National Council of the Churches of Christ in the United States of America.

Scripture quotations marked KJV are from the King James Version of the Bible.

Copyright © 2020 by Steve Cioccolanti

*All rights reserved*

Paperback ISBN (Third Edition): 978-1-922273-17-8

Ebook ISBN: 978-0-9804839-8-7

*Printed in the U.S.A.*

# CONTENTS

*Forewords*                                                    ix
*Preface About Language*                                       xiii
*Introduction*                                                 xv

Part I
UNDERSTANDING BUDDHISM
1. A Story from Behind the Bamboo Curtain                       3
2. The Story of the Eel                                         4
3. East Meets West                                             9
4. The Thin Buddha, Fat Buddha & Laughing Buddha              14
5. Who Was Buddha?                                            17
6. The Lotus Parable                                          21
7. The Teachings of Buddha                                    25
8. The Four Noble Truths                                      27
9. The Polio Victim                                           38
10. How Jesus Made Himself Known                              45
11. The Five Commandments of Buddha                           51
12. What Would Jesus Say to Buddhists?                        56
13. The Korean Buddhist                                       62
14. The Ten Karmas                                            68
15. Is There a Hell?                                          71
16. Reincarnation                                             80
17. Women in Buddhism                                         89
18. King Asoka & the Python                                   92
19. Jesus On Reincarnation                                    97
20. The King & The Ungrateful Debtor                         101
21. The Blind Turtle                                         110
22. The Last Words of Buddha                                 112
23. Which Denomination?                                      129
24. The Three Baskets (Tripitaka)                            139
25. The Six Buddhist Councils                                148
26. King Naresuan                                            151

27. Summary 157
28. End Time Predictions of Buddha & Jesus 162

Part II
CHRISTIAN QUESTIONS
29. The Authority of the Bible 175
30. The Validity of Buddhist Stories 179
31. The Risk of Syncretism 182
32. Is Buddha in Heaven? 186
33. The Last Words of Jesus 189
34. What Would Buddha Say? 197

*Appendix* 199
*Notes* 203
*Other Books by Steve Cioccolanti* 216
*Videos by Steve Cioccolanti* 218
*Meet Steve Cioccolanti* 221

# FOREWORDS

You have in your hands a groundbreaking book, one that will challenge you to rethink our faith and how it can reach those whom others have overlooked.

I was raised in Hawaii, a blending of the East and West. My mother was for many years of her life a Buddhist. My father was Catholic, so I grew up confused! I was in caught between the two cultures and the two beliefs of those I loved.

As I came to know Christ in my late teenage years, I developed a heart to reach those of other faiths. I quickly learned that the first step to that goal was not necessarily sharing the Four Spiritual Laws or by giving them a copy of the New Testament. Rather, it was to understand their perspective and loving each one as a person for whom Christ died.

Having read Steve Cioccolanti's courageous work, I was challenged afresh and stirred in my heart to now confidently take the next step in reaching Buddhists with the Gospel. It teaches the reader how with understanding and context, we can build Goodwill, which one day will open a doorway for the Good News!

Steve Cioccolanti is a sincere follower of Christ with an unusual insight into the Buddhist mind. His background and context lends to a broad understanding that no causal college can bring to any avid student of life. You will hear his compassion as well as his comprehension for those who have been raised within generations of Buddhist traditions and beliefs. He will even challenge you to see the good in it rather than just the bad. You will view the elements that have drawn millions in Asia and beyond to a philosophy of life that has withstood millennia of criticism and wars.

I have recommended this book to our Bible College students as they attempt to reach the Pacific Rim. I recommend it to you as you go forward to reach your world for Christ.

—DR. WAYNE CORDEIRO
President of Pacific Rim Bible College
Pastor of New Hope Christian Fellowship, Hawaii

In Australia, the 2006 Census tells us that the number of Buddhists has grown by 107% since 1996. However it seems there has been little growth in understanding Buddhism within the Church or by Christians generally.

Some parts of the Church have adopted Buddhist meditation practices. Some see it as a religion of peace, promoting tolerance and self-understanding, not much different from Christianity. The Buddhist concepts of karma and reincarnation are accepted by a surprising number of young people, including many in the Church.

In his excellent book, Steve Cioccolanti provides a very welcome window into Buddhism as someone who has been on the inside. Through Buddhist stories and legends, he opens up the teachings of Buddha that are often more about a search for life than pathways to hope and fulfillment. He includes a description of the different variations of Buddhism from different countries, and issues such as women in Buddhism and "Is Buddha in Heaven?"

The surprising features of this book are not only the candid information about Buddhism, but also the way Steve intertwines this with the Christian message of hope - comparing Buddhist teachings with the Bible, presenting some of the key Buddhist symbols as doorways to eternal life in Christ, and asking personal questions of the reader about their own beliefs, with prayers they can pray for enlightenment.

This is a book that would be of great value to any Christian seeking information about Eastern religions, especially if wanting to share their faith with a Buddhist. It would also be valuable and readable for a Buddhist person to understand their own faith, and to gain an understanding of Jesus.

—REV. ROB ISAACHSEN
Founder of Transforming Melbourne

# PREFACE ABOUT LANGUAGE

It is inevitable that you will learn a few new words as you find out more about Buddhism. For instance, the word *Buddha* is not an English word. It is a Sanskrit word from the root *budh* which means to awaken. Hence Buddha means the "awakened one" or the "enlightened one". There are many other foreign words you would have to learn if you want to study Buddhism, which creates a language barrier for the average person (even Buddhist!).

If you want to study deeply about Buddhism (and I'm not assuming you do), you will need to learn two foreign and ancient languages, *Pali* and *Sanskrit*. Muslims will understand this as they have a similar belief. If you want to become a serious Muslim, you are supposed to read the Koran in Arabic. Many Muslims who do not speak Arabic just recite the Arabic sounds without knowing the meaning. Buddhists do the same thing by chanting in the ancient languages of India which they do not understand.

Christianity in Europe used to have a similar problem when the Bible was written only in Latin[1]. However, the Protestant Reformation[2] led to the translation of the Bible into native languages[3]. Catholics did not permit the use of the vernacular but continued to conduct masses in Latin up until 1965![4]

Till today, Buddhists do not translate every Buddhist word into their native language. For instance, the word "karma" comes directly from Pali-Sanskrit[5]. Other words such as "the cycle of reincarnation" are nearly always translated, because few people would recognize the word in its original Pali-Sanskrit form, which is "samsara".

If you need time to absorb the new words, don't be surprised! Almost no one speaks Pali-Sanskrit today; they are ancient languages like Latin or classical Greek. Ancient Buddhist words will be repeated in their modern English and Thai forms, since 60 million Buddhists currently speak Thai. In Thai, the word "karma" is pronounced "gumma" or simply truncated in everyday speech to "gum" (rhymes with "hum"). You can pronounce any Buddhist word in English, in Thai or in Pali-Sanskrit. Throughout this book, you will find key words in their alternative forms because it's a bit of education that will help you in cross-cultural understanding and communication.

To appreciate the influence of Pali-Sanskrit language on Buddhist culture, a Westerner need only compare it to the impact of Greco-Roman language on Western civilization. Imagine a university student trying to successfully qualify as a doctor, lawyer, biologist, chemist or astronomer without learning any new Greek or Latin words! She needs not speak Latin or Greek, but she needs to be comfortable with the terms of her trade. Similarly, to be Buddhist or understand Buddhism, you need to learn some of these ancient words.

Words are free, and more importantly, words build bridges, so please enjoy learning a few new words!

# INTRODUCTION

I will not assume you know Buddhism. I will walk you through the basics. My main aim is to help Christians understand Buddhism the way it's actually lived, not the way it's taught in textbooks. When Christians talk to Buddhists, you should not feel as if they are against Christ or they are "closed" to the Gospel. Not necessarily. That's what I would like to help you understand. While there are some differences, there are also many striking similarities.

So why should we be interested in Buddhism?

Buddhism is the state or majority religion of 12 countries: Bhutan, Cambodia, China, Japan, Laos, Mongolia, Myanmar, South Korea, Sri Lanka, Thailand, Tibet, and Vietnam. Buddhism is also very important culturally in several other regions of the world such as India, Indonesia, Singapore, Taiwan and Hawaii[1]. Today at least 350 million people are born Buddhists. That's equivalent in size to the entire population of the United States or half of all Europeans alive today! While most Buddhists were born into Buddhist families, some Westerners are studying and/or converting to Buddhism. Besides that, many people in the world are taking up an interest in martial arts, and 90% of all Oriental martial arts is heavily influenced by Buddhism. So it is relevant for us – Christians, Buddhists, and others – to talk about Buddhism.

As for me, there are many reasons why I love Buddhists. I grew up in a Buddhist country, I received Buddhist teachings, and I have Buddhists in my family. When I used to call myself a deist, I wore around my neck a white Buddha and a Jerusalem cross. Interestingly, while I was in my native Buddhist country, several Buddhist-background believers persuaded me to consider more personally Christianity. Therefore I look at Christianity from Eastern eyes, and I have come to embrace Christ for myself.

But since I have spent some time in the West, namely Australia, different states in America and different nations in Europe, I also have a perspective on Western thinking. I believe that Western intellectuals currently do not understand Buddhism. They explain it in terms of tolerance, harmony and cosmic unity, which I think sells well to the Western public, but if I ever heard any of those terms used by a Buddhist while I was growing up, I cannot recall one instance!

To many Western intellectuals, I suspect, Buddhism may serve as a reaction against something they dislike, namely Christianity. The truth is, Buddhism is not a reaction against Christianity. Christianity didn't even exist at the time Buddha was around!

When a person comes from that paradigm – in which they are reacting to the Christian traditions they dislike and they adopt Buddhism – they really do not understand what it's about. That is actually part of the appeal to Westerners. It is probably the main appeal amongst scholars, students, and New Agers. The appeal of Buddhism is the mystery of what they don't understand.

In this book, I am going to explain to you aspects of Buddhism in a way that native Buddhists would easily understand, but in a way that you are not likely to ever hear in a Western classroom. You will also learn about the similarities between Christianity and Buddhism that may be unexpected, and read about many real life stories. The lives of modern Buddhists comprise one of the great untold stories of spiritual literature.

I am aware that there are hundreds of books on Buddhism, and similar resources on Christianity. Where my efforts come in is not to repeat or replace their works, but to fill in the gaps and to emphasize certain things that have long been neglected in the available literature No doubt many authors (both native and foreign) have attempted to shed light on these great faiths separately. The gap which remains, it seems to me, is no insider has attempted to bring understanding to both faiths simultaneously. I have been Buddhist and now I am Christian. I have lived with Buddhists and Christians. What I will share will be not be theoretical, but real facts and true stories from an insider's perspective.

There are a lot of reasons to study these two Great Religions of the World – Buddhism and Christianity, and to study them together! After reading this book, its facts, its *never-before-translated* parables, and its real life stories of Buddhists and Christians, you will no longer have to wonder about these two great faiths! At least you should be more open to converse with the next Buddhist (or Christian) you meet.

# PART I
# UNDERSTANDING
# BUDDHISM

# A STORY FROM BEHIND THE BAMBOO CURTAIN

The term "iron curtain" referred to an invisible, ideological wall that separated Eastern (communist) Europe from Western Europe. For nearly 50 years, people inside the communist bloc did not fully know or understand what was happening in the rest of the world. They perceived the West as their enemy. Through much prayer this wall came down, as symbolized by the tearing down of the Berlin Wall in 1989.

A similar invisible wall separates Christians from Buddhists, which I will call the "bamboo curtain". Non-Buddhists don't really understand what's going on inside Buddhist cultures, Buddhist families and Buddhist lives. And most Buddhists also don't really know what Christianity or the Bible is all about. They sometimes perceive each other as enemies, which is simply not the case.

There are many stories I wish I could tell you, but time and space limits us. We will begin with one. More will come later in this book. *The Story of the Eel* will give you a peek into what it is really like to be born in a Buddhist country and to live as a Buddhist.

## 2
## THE STORY OF THE EEL

This story is not intended for children. It's an adult story, so I will try to word it delicately so the adults will understand. In this account I will show you how the doctrine of **karma** works in real life.

I travel regularly to Thailand for public speaking and on one of my trips I sat down with a Buddhist friend. This is what she told me.

Since the age of 12, I could not say the word "eel"[1]. I could not even stand to hear the word eel. I would literally go into shock. My father once tried to fry some eel and that was the last time. My entire family could not eat eel[2] any more.

My husband of eight years had the job of holding the remote control in his hands while watching TV, just in case the word eel was ever spoken. When we went to the market together, he had to hold my arm just in case we saw an eel in the marketplace. What happened to me?

When I was 12 years old, I ran to Watergate Market[3] and I witnessed an eel go up a merchant woman's skirt. The woman screamed in pain and tried to pull the eel out but the eel bit her. Both the woman and the eel died with blood everywhere. This was in the newspaper 30 years ago.

This incident sunk into my memory and every time I heard or saw another eel, I would literally fall over and shake like an epileptic. According to Buddhism, this is a karma that had followed me from my past life of sins. Thai Buddhists call this *wain gum* or the revenge of karma. Other Buddhists explained to me that in a past life, I must have done something wrong to an eel, so now in this life the eel must do something to me. Our belief is that karma always follows us. It will follow us forever until somehow it is paid for.

I went to the temple and sought a monk's help. This is what he advised me, "You must first meditate, then *sadau kro*[4]. To do this, you must release 99 eels in 99 temples." I was so afraid. Normally if I only saw one eel I would pass out and faint. The monk told me to release 99! I was so afraid that I brought a friend to hold the bucket carrying the 99 eels while I held on to her hand. I shook all over just holding on to my friend's hand. My friend and I released all 99 eels in one single temple, so I wondered if it counted or if I had really cheated.

The monk said, "If you cannot do it, then become a nun[5] to pay off your sins." This meant I had to stay in the temple, wear white, sleep on a mat, eat 2 meals a day, walk in circles, and think about breathing in and breathing out, and which foot I was going to take the next step with. I could only do this for 2 months.

Did it work? It didn't change a thing! I still could not bear to hear or utter the word eel.

At that time I owned a restaurant which a Christian happened to rent from me. Two years earlier this Christian renter tried to evangelize me and she told me the news about God. But she told me in the wrong way. She said, "Do you want to come to church? Coming to church is good. Being a Christian is good." She said, "If you do wrong or sin, if you cuss anyone or blame anyone or steal anything from anyone, then on Sunday you can go to church and confess your sins

and it's all gone. The next week you can start sinning again!"
I became scared of her and avoided her. I would not go to her
church. My husband, however, went twice.

When this lady asked me the third time and I refused, she
cussed me out. From that point on, I hated Christians. It
became a passion in me. I wanted to know if Christianity
teaches people to be like her. What type of God teaches
people to be bad?

I developed a drive to know what Christianity was really
like. So whenever I sat in a taxi and did not see any idols[6], I
would ask, "Are you a Christian? Can you explain
Christianity to me?" but not one of them could. One day a
relative told me, "I'm a Christian now!" I told my husband
we shouldn't spend any more time with her. I did not want to
be evangelized.

My relative kept asking me to church. Finally out of
respect for my family, I decided to go to her church. The first
morning I came to church, both my husband and I were still
hung over from the night before. We drank every opportunity
we saw beer. We were beer-oholics. I was sent into the new
believer's room and the minister said, "Pray and dare to ask
God for anything! Dare to ask God to show you that He is
real." So I closed my eyes and as I began to pray, I felt like I
was levitating. This happened three times but I still would
not believe. Maybe I imagined it, I thought.

Nonetheless I wanted to come back to church on
Wednesday. And I came drunk again. I asked for the pastor to
pray for me, then I went home and continued to meditate as I
always did. But something had begun to change. I didn't
want to chant in Pali any more, so my husband had to chant
by himself. I wanted to go to church.

As I did, I could feel deep down in my heart that I was
becoming a more peaceful person. I became a kinder person.
I lost my temper less. Pretty soon I started inviting my
husband to come to church with me regularly.

My life had changed through attending church, so I decided to get water baptized. It was then that a miracle happened. One day my husband was watching TV and he forgot to press the remote control when someone said "eel". He was so scared that I would pass out. But I hadn't taken any notice. He said, "Honey, didn't you hear they said eel?" I said, "Did they say eel?" My husband was even more shocked, "What? You can say eel, too?!"

This is how we knew that I had been released from all karma. It didn't follow me anymore. There was no more *wain gum* following me for my past sins. After I could say eel for about two months, I was so happy I went to visit my mother who was 84 years old. I told her, "Mother, I can say eel now!" My mother was so happy she asked me, "Can I come to church with you?" She came and Jesus healed her of kidney stones. The doctors had previously told her that she did not have long to live. But after that service he took an x-ray of her and there was no evidence of any stones left!

This is one of the many stories of Buddhists I could tell you. This is the doctrine of karma in real life, not in textbooks. If you have a fear of eels, it is assumed you once hurt an eel. If you were born or became a paralytic, it is assumed you had been bad in a previous life. **Karma is always retributive.**

The self-blame, the fear of karmic revenge, the hopelessness of never being set free from a curse, all add stress and uncertainty to a Buddhist life. Please don't think that the typical Buddhist is living in harmony with nature or floating on a cloud of peace and that they don't need to hear the Gospel that Christians have to share with them.

The doctrine of karma does not usually produce compassion, but condemnation. When sincere Buddhists try to purify themselves of their own karma, and keep all 227 laws of Buddha (for men), they realize they cannot do it. This produces even more condemnation.

The Story of the Eel is our first illustration of how Western assumptions so often clash with Eastern realities.

# 3

# EAST MEETS WEST

Do all Buddhists emphasize reincarnation, practice meditation and consider self to be an empty illusion? Western perception of Buddhism would seem to suggest so. In reality many Buddhist don't talk about reincarnation, but of going to Heaven or Hell. Few Buddhists practice meditation regularly. And most Buddhists love life and making money.

Do Buddhists worship Buddha as their god? This is another cross-cultural misunderstanding. Some Christians have assumed that "Buddhists think Buddha is god just like Christians think Jesus is God." Buddhists, in fact, think that Buddha was a human being, albeit a very special human being.

The misunderstanding cuts both ways. Some Buddhists have assumed that "Jesus was the leader of the Christian religion; just like Buddha was the leader of the Buddhist religion." Christians, to be clear, believe that Jesus is far more than a religious leader, but in fact the Creator God who came in the flesh. Whereas Buddha never commanded anyone to worship Buddha; Jesus accepted worship[1] and said

anyone who believed Him to be the Savior would have
eternal life[2].

## Dispelling the Myths

W hy do so many misunderstandings about Buddhism
continue to abound in this so-called "Information
Age"? I can suggest three out of possibly many reasons.

F irst, doctrine is simply not as important to a Buddhist
as practice. By practice, I mean that a typical Buddhist
may spend her whole life participating in the rites, chants
and symbolism of Buddhism without ever once questioning
her religion intellectually. This is almost impossible to a
Western mind.

The Westerner wants a clearly defined set of consistent
beliefs. The Buddhist is mainly preoccupied with traditional
practices. The fact that these practices may have been
developed before Buddha or after Buddha, or been adopted
from Hinduism or animism, or contradict some teachings of
Buddha himself, is of little import to her.

The average Buddhist is not always consistent in her
beliefs. For instance, she may believe in both reincarnation
AND Heaven and Hell – this is confusing to the Westerner.
Buddhists believe that Buddha went to nirvana[3] which means
he disappeared out of existence, yet they pray to him. "Who
are they praying to?" the Westerner might want to know. The
typical Buddhist has rarely given such contradiction a
thought.

The concept of "luck"[4] is very important to most
Buddhists. Buddha images are thought to bring their owners
good luck. In Asia many people wear small Buddha amulets

because they feel it will bring them luck. Yet Buddha's own teachings can be interpreted as to rule out the existence of luck. "The Law of Causation" (as taught by Buddha) says nothing happens randomly or by chance.

Buddhism prides itself as a religion based on reason. If everything is based on cause and effect, as Buddha taught, then there can be no possibility of luck. Yet most Buddhists live in deep-seated fear of bad luck[5] and will buy as many idols as they think will protect them from bad luck and attract good luck. The intellectual Westerner sees this as a contradiction: either believe in superstition or believe in logic; but one should not believe in both! Easterners are not so consistent in their theory. This makes it very hard for Westerners to follow and understand.

**Religion to a Buddhist is a set of practices, not a set of answers.** To a Westerner, the typical Buddhist is strangely unquestioning. Buddhism does not answer the questions of the origin of the universe, the origin of demons, the origin of mankind, the beginning or ending of karma. It merely states that karma comes from our inward lusts, but it doesn't tell us *why* we have them. For a religion that believes in the law of causation, the causes of significant things are overlooked, and the issue of a "First Cause" is completely ignored!

If the universe is the result of cause and effect, a Western mind typically demands the answer to an obvious question: "Who or What was the *First* Cause?" To believe that the universe had no beginning has been proven false.[6] To believe the universe's beginning had no cause is illogical. Everything that has a beginning must have a cause. The universe needs a cause.

The Buddhist theory of "karmic law" sounds so similar to the Western scientific law of cause and effect. This is both its appeal and its turn off to Westerners. On the one hand, some Westerners are attracted to the idea that Buddhism seems like a "scientific religion". On the other hand, most

Westerners cannot accept a religion that is silent on the origin, purpose and destiny of life. The Biblical account of Creation fills a gap that Buddhism leaves wide open. To believe a Personal, Intelligent, Moral God started time and space is sensible to the mind and rings true to the heart. Evidence shows there is intelligent and intricate design on every level of the universe, even though it is fallen and fast-decaying due to our sins.

My purpose is not to reveal logical contradictions in Buddhism, nor is it to compare the differences between Buddhism and Christianity. What I intend to emphasize are the many largely unrecognized similarities between Buddhism and Christianity, which can serve as a starting point for cross-cultural communication. Yet I will be clear about what the differences between Buddhism and Christianity are.

I touch on some Buddhist inconsistencies only to help explain why Buddhism has been hard to "pin down" to a set of consistent beliefs. Easterners are typically not as analytical as Westerners. Westerners tend to use arguments. Westerners like to debate such questions as, "Did Jesus exist?" Easterners never ask, "Did Buddha exist?" His *10 times* existence goes unquestioned, though certainly much harder to prove than Christ's single and very public life.

I will try to present Buddhist beliefs in a way that makes sense to someone with a Western and/or Christian frame of mind. I will also try to pinpoint the core beliefs and practices of Buddhism that are the bare essentials relevant to evangelism.

The second reason Westerners tend to get a muddied picture of Buddhism is that those Westerners who are most likely to become interested in Buddhism have usually had some unpleasant childhood experience in a Christian church and view Buddhism as a rejection of what they disliked about their church experience. Tainted with such a view, some Western seekers may subconsciously want Buddhism to be something it historically is not.

In the West Buddhism has become a privatized religion based on careless individualism. It is perceived as a boundless, rule-less, "free my own mind" religion. Though there are many disagreements within Buddhism, the one thing it is NOT is "whatever I want it to be". What is Buddhism? The answer must be posed in the form of a question: "What did Buddha want it to be?" That's Buddhism. That's one of the primary subjects of this book.

The third reason may be attributed to the Western popularization of the Dalai Lama, who represents a small but widely publicized sect of Buddhism in China-controlled Tibet. Tibetan Buddhism is the latest form of Buddhism, developing separately in Tibet around 7th to 8th century AD. Tibetan Buddhism or Lamaism believes that a Buddha died but keeps coming back in the form of a Dalai Lama. It has probably contributed more to Western popularization of the concept of reincarnation than any other factor. But we must ask, "Was the original Sakyamuni Buddha a Tibetan Buddhist?" From the viewpoints of geography and history, the answer is no. I will touch on the concept and misconceptions of reincarnation throughout this book.

I intend to show you that by looking honestly at historical Buddhism and historical Christianity, you will find that the two are not at odds, but one leads to the other – the older paves the way to the younger. The last words of Buddha open up to the first words of Christ in the New Testament.

# 4

# THE THIN BUDDHA, FAT BUDDHA & LAUGHING BUDDHA

Many people have wondered, "How come Buddha looks so different in various temples? Is he fat or is he skinny? Is he serious or is he funny?" People are not sure.

When you see some of the old statues of Buddha, he looks like a thin man. When you go up to Japan, he looks like Hercules, a big muscular man. When you come down to Thailand, he's reclining and serene. Go over to China and he has a pot belly and is laughing away. They call him the Laughing Buddha. But go to Tibet and you'll see he's very serious and stern. Come back down to Vietnam and he's thin again.

People look at all this and say, "Which one is he? Which Buddha is the real Buddha?" Just as Buddhism varies from country to country, so too Buddha looks different in each country.

So was Buddha thin or fat? Tradition says that Buddha only ate one meal a day. He was an ascetic who lived a very sparse life in the forest for up to six

years. Your guess is as good as mine as to what he physically looked like, but if you ate one meal a day you probably would not be so big. At least I don't think you would have a pot belly. In fact, the pot belly Buddha is a different person, not the original Sakyamuni Buddha. The laughing Buddha was a monk named *Hotei* who is predicted in Mahayana[1] Buddhism to be a returning or end times Buddha, called the *Maitreya*[2].

Was Buddha serious or funny? If you go back to the early Buddhist teaching, you will find that Buddhism was actually opposed to humour and laughter. Out of the 227 rules for monks which are recorded in the *Vinaya*, one of the rules stipulates no loud laughter. It is a sin to laugh so that other people can hear you. Again, I would not be dogmatic about it, but it seems the original Buddha would have been a slightly more serious person than later depictions of him.

## THE DIVERSITY OF BUDDHISM

Buddhism is as diverse as Christianity. Buddhist devotees all around the world differ in their practices. Some monks shave their eyebrows, some don't. Some monks can have wives, some can't. (This is similar to Christianity: Catholic priests can't marry, Protestant pastors can.[3]) Some wear orange robes, some green, others don yellow or white. Some can wear shoes, some can't wear shoes. Some can carry money, some can't carry money. Some teach reincarnation, some believe in Heaven and Hell. Some believe in the *Dalai Lama* who keeps coming back again and again - the present one being the 14<sup>th</sup> Dalai Lama. Some believe in a prophetic end time Buddha; in other words, Buddha has come once, but Buddha is coming again, and his name is called *Maitreya*. Some believe that Buddha will never come again. The fact that he is a "Buddha" means it is the last time he came and he will not be born another time.

One reason Buddhists don't agree on theology and practice is that they do not have one agreed text (like the Bible) and the existing texts are voluminous. (We will examine the main Buddhist texts in the chapter called *The Three Baskets.*) All of this diversity makes it very difficult to pin point exactly what Buddhism is or to make universal statements about what every single Buddhist believes. There are so many different ways people practice it.

But neither is Buddhism a free-for-all. We will start with what everybody virtually agrees on – the life of Buddha – then cover the absolutely fundamental teachings of Buddha on the 4 noble truths, 5 moral laws, 10 karmas, and reincarnation, before exploring the rarely translated parables and prophecies of Buddha.

5

# WHO WAS BUDDHA?

Who was the historical Buddha? His name was not Buddha, but Siddhartha Gautama. He was an Indian prince who searched for the way to escape karma. He is also known by the title *Sakyamuni*, which means the "Sage of the Sakya clan".

**Siddhartha Gautama** is held to be the 10th and last reincarnation of the same person. Strictly speaking, once someone has achieved buddhahood, he or she is not supposed to come back. Yet there are some Buddhists who are expecting the *Maitriya* or an End Times Buddha to come back[1] and there are some Buddhists who believe that the *Dalai Lama* is a buddha come back. However, when we speak of Buddha, we will be referring to the Gautama Buddha, the one who declared, "This is the last time I will be born."

(To distinguish him from other buddhas, it is customary to refer to Gautama as the Sakyamuni Buddha.)

Buddha was born on April 8 in Lumpini Park[2], a garden in ancient India or present day Nepal. Seven days later his mother Queen *Maya* died. He was subsequently raised by his mother's younger sister *Maha-prajapati*. Five days after birth his father King *Suddhodana* received a prophecy from 8 brahmins[3] that Siddhartha had the potential to become a great man. Asita said, "If he does not become a great holy man, he will become a great king. If he becomes a holy man, he will become the greatest founder of the greatest religion in the world." But the youngest of the *brahmins* named *Gaundinya*[4] spoke up and said, "No, he must become a monk and he will become enlightened and the founder of a great religion."

His father, being a king, understandably did not like the idea of his son becoming a monk, so he decided to shield his son from religious teachings and the knowledge of human suffering. He tried to make him enjoy comfort and only see the pleasures of life. In fact, he built 3 palaces for his young son so he could be comfortable during each of the 3 seasons of the year[5].

At the age of 16 he married a young princess, a cousin[6] named *Yasotara*. They were married for 13 years. At the age of 29, he had his first and only son named *Rahula* or *Rahun* in Thai.

It was around this time that the Prince left his palace and saw four different people: an elderly person, a sick person, a dead person and lastly a priest. He saw that after humans are born, they suffer from old age, illness, and death. The thought came to him that everybody suffers and no one could escape the suffering. This was the problem that troubled his heart, he thought about this over and over. He wanted a way out of this vicious cycle – the "wheel of suffering".

Then he thought that in life there is duality. If there's hot, there's cold. If there's suffering (birth, aging, sickness, death), then there must be something opposite (no birth, no suffering, no pain, no death). The prince saw the happiness of the world as an illusion[7] and the true purpose of life is to escape the cycle of suffering. The only way to escape the cycle of suffering is to be liberated[8] from the cycle of life.

He considered that one way to achieve this was to become celibate and a monk. So at the age of 29 he abandoned his newborn baby *Rahula* and his wife *Yasotara*. At first he made a decision to become a *sadhu*, or a monk within the Hindu religion. He cut his hair, changed his clothes, and changed his status from being a very rich person to becoming a very poor person. Whatever he had remaining he gave to his servant *Channa* to take home. He tried to follow two Hindu *brahman* teachers but felt Hinduism did not provide the answer[9]. He left to find his own way.

Soon he had five disciples following him. After 6 years of living as an ascetic in the forest, punishing his body, fasting, praying, and meditating, he gave up. He went bathing in a river and accepted a bowl of milk pudding from a woman named *Sujata*[10]. At this his five disciples were very shocked. Sorely disappointed, they left him.

Alone, Siddhartha continued his search for a way out of the cycle of suffering, choosing a more moderate path. Legend has it that he sat under a fig tree[11] and vowed not to get up until he was enlightened. At the age of 35, he became enlightened.[12] This historically meant the divide of Hinduism and Buddhism. Buddha actually split from the Hindu tradition and the teachings of the *brahmans* and started a new religion.

A Bodhi tree or Bo tree.

Buddha's teaching career began as he sought out two of his original teachers to share what he had found, but as it turned out they were both dead. He remembered his five original disciples. He found them and taught them, but only one understood what he was saying. It was actually the young *brahmin* who had insisted at Siddhartha's birth that he must become a Buddha. Thus *Gaundinya* became the first enlightened Buddhist disciple[13].

After some time, all 5 disciples succeeded in becoming enlightened and constituted the first company of Buddhist monks[14]. These five helped spread the teachings they had learned from Buddha.

# 6

## THE LOTUS PARABLE

As Buddha started preaching his message, he became disappointed and somewhat lost heart as he realized that he may not be able to reach everyone with his teaching. So he came up with a parable that divided humanity into four groups. He said people are like lotuses, some are above water, some are at the same level as the water, some are just underneath the water and some are all the way down at the bottom of the river, in the mud and clay. What was Buddha saying?

Basically he was explaining the degree of open-mindedness of people. Some people are like the lotus that is above water: they are smart people who can listen and learn and grow. Some are like a lotus that is on the same level as the water: these people have average intelligence, if they listen and continue to practice, they will understand. Some people are like a lotus under water: they have little intelligence; it takes them a long time, a lot of effort and a lot of practice to learn. Then some people are like a lotus in the mud: they are idiots – ignorant and unwilling to learn. No matter how much they hear, they will not understand. There is no chance of them coming up out of the water. That's how Buddha saw the world.

This parable is quite similar to the "Parable of the Sower" that Jesus taught. Isn't it true that Jesus also divided His listeners into four groups? He said the words that God speaks are like seeds, and the hearts of his listeners are like four types of soil. When God's truth is sown into the soil of the human heart, it will reveal the condition of the heart. Jesus said only one out of four will be good ground for God's Word; that is, when they hear the truth, they allow the truth to change their hearts and their minds, and their lives begin to produce fruit as God intended. The other three will respond different: some will be apathetic and indifferent; some will get excited temporarily but quit under pressure; some will follow a few steps then get distracted by worldly pursuits. Three out of four listeners will receive perfectly good seed, but not act on it, and not yield any harvest.

This was clearly illustrated when the Resurrected Christ told 500 of His disciples[1] face-to-face, "Go wait for the outpouring of the Holy Spirit," yet ten days later how many were actually obedient? Only a hundred and twenty.[2] That was a quarter of the people Jesus invited. Apparently three quarters of Jesus' own disciples had other things to do than to receive the Holy Spirit, speak in tongues and be mocked for Jesus on the Day of Pentecost!


BUDDHA'S HEART FOR TRUTH

When we compare Buddha's words with Jesus' words, we find that Buddha really had some insights that were pretty amazing. Buddha identified four types of students in the Parable of the Lotus. Christ divided his hearers into four groups in the Parable of the Sower (Matthew 13, Mark 4, Luke 8). It is only 2000 years later that knowledge of the 4 main types of personalities has become mainstream!

Christian authors such as Florence Littauer and Tim LaHaye have written several books on the importance of recognizing the four personalities. Christian counsellor Gary Smalley defines the four personalities as: lion; otter; beaver; and golden retriever. Secular leadership and management consultants define the four personalities as: Dominant; Influential; Steady and Compliant (DISC). This knowledge is now used in marital and pre-marital counselling of couples and by recruitment agencies to identify how an employee might respond to challenges, influence others, respond to rules and procedures, and adapt to change.

What Buddha alluded to in one parable, God amplified to the full in the New Testament. The New Testament is the only major account of God to be written from four different perspectives (Matthew, Mark, Luke, and John) – it is Good News written for all personalities, all soils, all lotuses![3]

Christians need to understand that while Buddha was not the Truth, Buddha was, in fact, a wise man. He sought for the Truth, and God promises, "If you seek Me, you will find Me."[4]

Is Buddha in Heaven today? Did Buddha find Christ? I don't want us to come to premature conclusions. We will draw on more evidence later. Suffice it to keep an open mind on the matter. The Bible says that God is a gracious God, and if you would seek for Him, there is a great possibility that you will find Him.

## BUDDHA'S RELIGIOUS VIEWS

Christians should be aware that Buddha was not against the pursuit of truth, even if it meant changing one's religion. Buddha never said you cannot change your religion. In fact, he abandoned his birth religion of Hinduism and changed to a new religion which eventually became known as Buddhism. So I don't believe Buddha would ever prohibit any Buddhist from exploring other truths in any other religion. He would not do that, and if he were alive today, I think he would probably be very happy to attend church and listen to the wisdom of the Bible. He simply did not have access to this most ancient testimony of truth. But Buddha was a very wise man and very open to learning.

The truth of Buddha's Lotus Parable bore itself out. According to Buddhist history, the number of people out of the entire world who finished their discipleship with Buddha and came to know as much as Buddha were only 60 people. Tradition claims that these 60 disciples went out to preach in 60 directions that did not overlap. Buddhism eventually reached as far north as Tibet, China, Mongolia, South Korea and Japan, and as far south as Sri Lanka. From Sri Lanka, Buddhism travelled to Myanmar, Cambodia, Thailand and Laos.

Buddhism never succeeded in parts of the world west of India, but managed to make initial inroads into Afghanistan. Today we may not think of Afghanistan as a Buddhist country (it is now Muslim), but up till 2002, there were giant Buddha statues that stood as a testament to the missionary efforts of early Buddhist disciples. Muslims have detonated the last remaining ones in Afghanistan and they are no longer there today.

Buddha's teaching career spanned across 45 years and he reached up to 2000 disciples.[5] These people did not become enlightened, they were not Buddha's themselves, but they were numbered among his converts. His favorite disciple was named *Ananda*.[6]

On a journey to the city of *Parva*, Buddha accepted some food offered by a blacksmith named *Chunda* and suffered food poisoning. He was ill for three months. In great pain, he died at the age of 80[7]. He lived from 563 B.C to 483 B.C[8].

# 7

# THE TEACHINGS OF BUDDHA

We have covered quickly Buddha's life and the history of Buddhism. Now we will look at Buddha's teachings.

Buddha did not teach anything against another religion or against Christianity in particular. Buddha was simply searching for a way out of this cycle of life. Buddha saw life as a revolving door of suffering and in his mind this was an imperfect condition which man needs to escape from. This was not an ideal state, but a fallen state of man.

Christians may need to ponder that. Doesn't that sound like what Jesus taught? The Bible agrees that man is suffering today and this is not what God wants for you and me. We have so many bridges between Christianity and Buddhism! Yet we don't talk to each other about them. And when we don't talk openly, we become separated from each other through ignorance. Out of ignorance comes prejudice. Efforts to engage in spiritual conversations seem to go no further than: "Hi, I'm Christian." "Well, I'm Buddhist." Finished. The conversation ends or changes topic.

But when we delve deeper, we share a lot in common and have a lot to talk about. I remember meeting a young

Buddhist student vacationing in Australia. When he found out that I was a Christian, he said, "I am Buddhist," and did not expect that I would carry on the conversation any further. But I love to hear someone say, "I am Buddhist," because I am interested in asking them questions about their faith, what they are practicing, where they are on their path, and how much success they are having in trying to escape suffering. Many Buddhists are interested to hear my story because I tell them I have found the way to escape suffering.

I don't treat Buddhists as strangers, nor do I treat Christians as aliens. I grew up with many religions around me. I believed in Buddhism, Catholicism, evolutionary science and various philosophies. I mixed them up together and made a religion to suit myself. My attitude was, "When I want to go to church, I'll go. When I want to go to mosque, I'll go. When I want to go to temple, I'll go. I decide what is true or not." I used to wear a silver Jerusalem cross and a beautiful white Buddha on the same necklace. I was very proud to have both of them on.

Eventually I realized that neither the cross nor the Buddha on my neck had any power to help me. What I really needed was what Buddha was searching for, and what Jesus had to offer – a way to escape the curses (Galatians 3:13). If a Buddhist were truly like Buddha, she would be trying to find a way to escape the curses that result from our accumulated karma. Buddha pointed to the way. Jesus said, "I am the Way" (John 14:6).

It's important to assure a Buddhist that having a relationship with Christ is not changing our nationality or changing our culture. We are pursuing a path that Buddha said for us to search for, which is to find the way, the truth and the life. Buddha did the Christian a great service by helping Buddhists understand that we are all morally fallen. How did Buddha teach this?

# 8

# THE FOUR NOBLE TRUTHS

Buddha taught four great truths[1]. Listen to these great truths and see if they sound similar to Christianity. Buddhists usually memorize these four truths in a foreign language, then they are taught the translation just like you will be right now.

**First Truth:** *tuk* or *tukka*[2]. Basically *tuk* means suffering. The first thing that Buddha taught was in life there is suffering. He saw sadness, fear, worry, disappointments, loneliness, people longing for loved ones gone and things that are lost. All this is suffering and everybody is in the same boat. That's what Buddha taught, no one is an exception.

**Second Truth:** *samuthai* or *samudaya*, which is the origin of suffering. Buddha discovered the cause of suffering. It is sin[3]. I believe the Bible completely agrees with this. Adam and Eve, the first man and woman God created, lived an ideal life and did not experience any suffering. God did not put them on earth to suffer. However, they had free will to love God or reject God. If they loved God, they would grow in an eternal relationship with their Creator. If they rejected God, they would die or be separated from the very Author of Life.

When Adam and Eve used their free will to trust in the devil
and rebel against God, then sin came into the world and into
their lives. Sickness, poverty and death were the results of
sin.[4] Every child that came out of Adam and Eve was born
with this sin nature and suffered the consequences of sin. Sin
is the cause of suffering. This is what the Book of Genesis
teaches.

Many Westerners have been taught that there is good
karma, bad karma, and neutral karma. This is not the normal
understanding of the average Buddhist. Karma is nearly
always synonymous with sin. It's that simple. We referred to
the Thai dictionary[5] and under the word karma or *gum*, we
found 3 definitions: (1) *gum* is "an action that sends evil to
the present and continues into the future"; (2) *gum* is "sin"[6];
(3) *gum* "can also mean death".

I love this third definition the most – sin is another word
for death! This lines up perfectly with Christian teaching.
Doesn't the Bible teach us in Romans chapter 6 verse 23 that
"the wages of sin is death"? The result of sin is death. The
price of sin is death. When you and I sin against God, we
deserve to die. Would Buddha agree? Well, the third
definition of *gum* is death!

In Thai we have an expression *terng gair gum* which means
"you have reached your karma." In other words, "it's time to
die". If you ever receive an invitation to a Thai funeral, it will
not read "So-and-So died" but "So-and-So *dai terng gai gum*."
Literally "they reached their *gum*" or they died. Karma results
in death. So the Buddhist concept of karma is very closely
related to the Christian concept of sin.

There is a fourth definition of karma in the Thai
Dictionary: "any action, work or deed." Theoretically that
could mean good, bad or neutral. Westerners really want to
focus on the last definition while ignoring the first three.
They would like to say, "I focus on building good karma
instead of suffering for my bad karma. I want to focus on my

action, works, or deeds, rather than my sins." That is not what Buddha is teaching. Sin (*gum*) is accumulated through the actions of our human nature. Since we are all sinners by nature or by birth[7], our actions are causing us to accumulate a lot of sins. So really you haven't changed anything by preferring the fourth definition.

## DID BUDDHA BELIEVE IN THE BASIC GOODNESS OF MAN?

Buddha taught that human nature is a sinful nature. Our "sin nature" is called *gilead tanha* in Thai. *Gilead* means anything that makes our hearts sad or unclean. Most Thai Buddhists are familiar with Buddha's description of various *gilead's*. There are 3 common *gilead's*: *lope, groed*, and *loeng*. *Lope* means greed, *groed* means anger, and *loeng* means delusion, deception, straying away, or not being willing to learn.

Buddha taught that these *gilead's* were part of the immoral nature of man. People are naturally greedy, angry and not willing to learn. The Bible agrees.

**ROMANS 7:14-17**

**14 For we know that the law is spiritual, but I am carnal, sold under sin.**

**15 For what I am doing, I do not understand. For what I will to do, that I do not practice; but what I hate, that I do.**

**16 If, then, I do what I will not to do, I agree with the law that it is good.**

**17 But now, it is no longer I who do it, but sin that dwells in me.**

Man's nature is not only full of *gilead*, it is also full of *tanha*. *Tanha* means lust. When Buddhists hear the word *tanha*, they usually think right away of sexual lust or sexual sins. So Buddha taught that man has an inward problem that cannot be fixed by an outward solution – *gilead tanha*. Because *gilead tanha* is locked inside human nature, people keep sinning and accumulating karma. Compare this to Paul's words:

### ROMANS 7:18-23

18 For I know that in me (that is, IN MY FLESH) NOTHING GOOD dwells; for to will is present with me, but how to perform what is good I do not find.

19 For the good that I will to do, I do not do; but the evil I will not to do, that I practice.

20 Now if I do what I will not to do, it is no longer I who do it, but SIN that DWELLS IN ME.

21 I find then a law, that EVIL IS PRESENT WITH ME, the one who wills to do good.

22 For I delight in the law of God according to the inward man.

23 But I see another law in my members, warring against the law of my mind, and bringing me into captivity to the law of SIN which is IN MY MEMBERS.

So far Buddha's teaching sounds a lot like Paul's preparation for the Gospel, doesn't it? Both are laying down solidly the foundation of humanity's problem, before building up to the solution.

I think Buddhism is really a friend to Christianity because it lays the ground work for the sinner's heart. If someone is a true Buddhist, she will realize, "I have a problem from which I cannot escape. I need to find help." And that is exactly what Jesus offers to do. He is our Helper because He is the only person born without *gilead tanha*. So He is able to rescue those with *gilead tanha* and those who have been burdened by the weight of karma.

### ROMANS 7:24-25

24 O wretched man that I am! Who will deliver me from this body of death?

25 I thank God-- through Jesus Christ our Lord! So

then, with the mind I myself serve the law of God, but
with the flesh the law of sin.

Jesus can deliver us out of the cycle of suffering. That's
what He said He could do.

MATTHEW 11:28

Come to Me, all you who labor and are heavy laden,
and I will give you rest.

The heaviness that every human heart feels is the weight
of sin, and its consequent guilt, fear and shame. If we try to
rid ourselves of that heaviness of heart through religious rule
keeping, it is hard labor! Jesus can lift us up, out from under
that hard labor and heavy load because although He was
tempted, He never succumbed to sin (Hebrews 4:15-16).

Let's review the Noble Truths so far.

The first truth was *tuk* or suffering.

The second truth was *samuthai*, the origin or cause of
suffering, which we found to be *karma* or sin.

**Third truth:** *nirod* or *nirodha*, which states that the end of
suffering should be attainable. Buddha invites us to ask the
question, "How to extinguish *tuk*?" Buddha basically taught
that the goal of life is to escape the *law of karma*[8]. We may
accomplish a lot of things in life, but if we miss this purpose
while we are yet alive, we will have missed the whole purpose
of life: to be set free from the law of karma and the continual
suffering karma would bring. That was the third truth.

**Fourth truth:** *mak* or *moksa*[9], which means the way to
escape. Buddha said there must be a way out, a way to escape
*karma* and *tuk*. Now the way that Buddha taught was very
similar to the way that Moses taught. It should not sound so
foreign to our ears. Buddha first taught Buddhists to try
disciplining the flesh.

The fourth noble truth led Buddha to create many rules to
try to curb the sins of human flesh. All of the rules deal only
with the flesh. Buddhism, in terms of practice, is all about

controlling the flesh. And that's virtually parallel to what Moses taught. Moses in effect said to the Jews, "Go ahead and try to control your flesh using these 613 commandments that God gave me." Honest Jews found out after a while, "There is no way I can do it. Everyday I break one or more of these commandments. I will never be free from sin!" Because many Jews came to this realization 2000 years ago, it was the perfect time for them to meet their Messiah or *Moksa*. Did Jesus not say in John chapter 14 verse 6, *"I am the way, the truth and the life, no man comes to the Father but by me"*?

Today Theravada Buddhists are in nearly the same situation that the Jews were in 2000 years ago. There is a densely populated area called South East Asia full of people who are fast coming to the self-realization, "I can't get away from sexual lust, I can't get away from anger, I can't get away from lying in business, I can't get away from all of these sins. According to Buddha, I am going to suffer, I am going to pay for all this, I am in big trouble!" That was the same sentiment many Jews felt when Jesus appeared in Israel 2000 years ago.

When Christians go to Southeast Asia and share Jesus Christ, we are not sharing something that is so foreign for those who truly understand Buddhism. We are sharing the very thing that every Buddhist is looking for. Buddhists who are truly following Buddha are looking for a way out of the "wheel of suffering." And that is why so many Buddhists are embracing and believing in Jesus Christ. We are able to follow the precepts of Buddha much better when we have Christ in our hearts. When we become born again Christians, we are no longer trying to discipline our flesh, but are granted a new nature with new desires in our hearts. The Holy Spirit who comes to live in us will help us, and we won't have to try to be better on our own. We simply can't do it.

When we come to this humble realization that we need

help, then we are in a position to ask Jesus to come into our hearts and God will help us change from the inside out. He will curb our poor attitude, solve our problems, and change what we don't like about our personalities. When we do wrong, He will correct us in a loving way and care for us like a good Father should.

## OBJECTION TO THE FATHER'S HELP

Initially, when hearing about God's grace for the first time, some Buddhists will insist that depending on someone else's help is a sign of weakness. They may resist the gift of God because they have not fully understood their own *gilead tanha* or the implications of Buddha's fourth noble truth called *mak*. They may think that they should try to help themselves.

Christians should not be daunted by this reply. This is really no different from a Westerner who refuses God's grace while claiming, "God helps those who help themselves," except a Buddhist may be in a better position to change because you can always refer them back to Buddha's fourth noble truth!

## OBEYING THE FOURTH NOBLE TRUTH

If you truly want to escape the curse of sin, Buddha said you must follow **311** rules if you are a woman (nun) and **227** rules if you are a man (monk). Buddha was a bit harder on women and easier on men, but those are the Buddhist rules as they stand. I would ask Buddhists who think they can help themselves to be honest, "Can you really keep all 227 rules?"

I cannot list all 227 rules here, but let us read some of the rules which according to Buddha could lead you to buddhahood if you kept them every day of your life. In other words, only by perfect obedience could you escape *karma* and reach *nirvana*[10]. Here are some of the rules that you must follow every day of your life to be good:

One unbreakable rule is: "No lying." Have you ever lied in your entire life? White lies, grey lies, black lies are all lies. Not keeping our word, lying to cover up our own shame, lying to our parents, lying to our spouse, even lying to make others feel good, are all lies. Everybody at some point in their life has lied. By this standard, you and I are already done for. We can't be a buddha anymore. But let's keep going.

"No insulting." Have you ever insulted anybody? I have! I didn't want to, but when I did, I had to receive payment for my karma through Jesus' blood on the cross.

"No tickling." This is one of the rules for a Buddhist monk!

"No putting arms akimbo." Westerners have a hard time understanding this as it seems a relaxed stance or posture of confidence, but it appears rude to most Asians. No arms akimbo in Asia!

"No playing in the waters." No more playing at the beach, body-boarding, surfing, swimming, snorkeling, scuba diving, etc.

"No bathing more than once every half a month, unless it is the last month of the hot season."

"No eating after noon."

"No traveling with a woman."

"No picking up anything valuable from off the street. Only if it's in your own house or in the temple, and you are picking it up for someone else to return it, then you may pick it up."

"No stuffing your mouth full until it is rounded." Have you ever been guilty of this?

"No speaking with the mouth full."

"No slurping." I just broke this one before writing this. I really try to be polite while I am drinking my soup, but occasionally I do slurp!

"No licking of hands, no licking of bowls, no licking of lips."

"No urinating while standing." All men reading, I am sorry to say, you have all broken this rule!

"No urinating on living trees."

"No urinating or spiting in water."

The list goes on and on. A true Buddhist monk will not even brush a mosquito away, but let it land on him and bite him. If you haven't done that all your life, you will have much *tuk* (suffering) in your life, according to Buddha's moral teaching.

If you can do all of the above (plus more!) consistently every day of your life, you may have hope of going to Heaven. But if you can't, you have absolutely no hope. It is hopeless, according to Buddha!

## THE MOSAIC SYSTEM

Buddha's excellent teaching to Asians carries the same heart as God's commandments to the Jews. If you can't keep all 613 commandments of God, you are a sinner. And if you are a sinner, you need a sin-sacrifice. That's why much of the Mosaic Law deals with the sacrificial system.

**LEVITICUS 17:11**

**For the LIFE of the flesh is IN THE BLOOD, and I have given IT [the blood] to you upon the altar to make atonement for your souls; for it is the BLOOD that makes ATONEMENT FOR THE SOUL.**

**HEBREWS 9:22**

**And according to the law almost all things are purified with blood, and WITHOUT SHEDDING OF BLOOD there is NO REMISSION [forgiveness of sins].**

This earthly system revealed to Moses foreshadowed the Coming Savior. Jews were supposed to understand the Savior' character and mission by seeing year after year an offering of the perfect lamb, the shedding of blood, the burning of the sacrifice – all depicting Jesus the Sinless Man, giving His blood on the Cross, and burning in Hell for 3 days. Our sins were transferred to the only One who has never sinned. Jesus voluntarily did that for us. He loves us that much.

The sacrificial system of the Old Testament proves that **man cannot help himself.** Only by repenting and believing in Jesus can we become righteous. To become righteous any other way is called in the Bible "self-righteousness". Self-righteous people ignore God's righteousness, bend the rules as they go, and justify themselves when they fail. This vain attempt to be self-righteous is the very opposite of a meek and humble spirit God loves, and is actually one of the worst sins God hates. The laws of Moses and the precepts of Buddha were meant to bring us to our knees and a humble realization of our desperate need for help.

## WHERE DO YOU STAND ON THE SCALE OF 'GOOD'?

All of us who have been tempted have at some point failed to pass the test. Our *gilead tanha* or sin nature compels us to do wrong, especially when we think we are doing it in secret or can get away with it.

Jesus is unique in that He was born without *gilead tanha*. He was born of a virgin. Being related to God the Father and not to our father Adam, Jesus inherited none of Adam's *gilead tanha*. Jesus chose to lead a pure life and never accumulated any *karma*. So Jesus is able to help those of us who have been tempted and gotten into trouble.
**HEBREWS 2:18**

For in that He Himself has suffered, being tempted, He is able to aid those who are tempted.

Jesus claims He is able to save the world!

**JOHN 12:47**

**... I did not come to judge the world but to save the world.**

It's up to you and me what we choose to do with that claim. Since Jesus taught me not to lie but to tell the truth, I would ask myself, "Why would Jesus lie if He were not able to save me? By telling me that He can forgive sins and guarantee eternal life, He had nothing to gain and His life to lose! Could it be that He said He could save the whole world, not to gain something, but because it's *true*?" These are amazing statements. The security I have in Christ's power to save me is the fact that He has never lied. Jesus always told the truth.

# 9

# THE POLIO VICTIM

## BECOMING A BUDDHA

In Buddhism, if you want to escape the cycle of suffering and go to Heaven, the qualification is that you become a Buddha[1]. A Buddha is someone who has been purified of karma, thereby passing out of the wheel of earthly life. If you're not a Buddha, then you are still stuck in the cycle of suffering along with the rest of humanity.

So what does it take to become a Buddha?

The first step is to *buad* or become a monk.

## WHY DO PEOPLE BECOME MONKS?

A Buddhist friend of mine used to go out to drink and party till he reached his 30s, at which point he started to realize, "I have really done a lot of bad things and have a lot of *wain gum* (karma). I had better do something about it!" His mother asked him to be a monk.

Around the same time, a Thai friend of his returned from Dubai and invited him to "be a monk for his mother".[2]

Westerners may think that Buddhists become monks for life, the way priests and pastors tend to serve in ministry all their lives. But to *buad* or become a monk is a way some Buddhists believe they can accumulate merits or *tam boon*. Many Thai males become a monk for 3 months at the age of 21. This is often "done for mum" to accumulate merit for her salvation. It is said that she will "hold on to the edge of the orange robe to lift her up to Heaven."[3]

When your father or mother dies, you can be a monk for 3-4 days. At funerals, someone in the family is expected to be a monk for a few days to send *boon* or merit to the dead. The intention is that the dead will deserve Heaven because of the extra merit earned, but there is no guarantee! It is a matter of blind faith.

A guilty conscience will also lead some males to become a monk temporarily. Whenever a Buddhist commits sin, he may try to ease his conscience by entering the monkhood. If as a monk he still does wrong (like looks at a woman, thinks about a woman, listens to music by mistake, or walks into a department store), he can *plong abad*. Once a week he has to sit and meditate[4], thinking on where he came from, thinking about his faults, and then confessing his sins to the senior monks. This is quite similar to the weekly confession for Catholics.

Additionally when a Buddhist feels "bad luck"[5] he may also wish to become a monk temporarily to accumulate better luck.

Being a monk is not the only way Buddhists try to accumulate merit or *tam boon*. You can *tam sangkatan* or give canned food, toothpaste, toothbrush, soap, and shaving kit to a monk. You can *tawai pain* or offer lunch to the monks. Any of these acts of *tam boon* only lessens[6] the sin, but never washes it away. It is important to note two things: (1) a person may *tam boon* all her life and not be guaranteed of escaping Hell, and (2) the main motivation of *tam boon* is a guilty conscience.

## QUALIFICATIONS FOR MONKHOOD

So at the age of 33, my friend accepted his friend's invitation to be a "monk for his mother". The two went to see a local monk and discussed the possibility of entering monkhood. The monk looked at him and said, "Your friend can be a monk, but you can't." "Why not?" he asked, surprised to be rejected. The monk told him because he had a physical deformity. He was "not complete in 32 parts."[7]

His body wasn't perfectly formed because when he was 8 years old he contracted polio; consequently his right leg grew smaller than his left one. In order to be a Buddha you must have a complete body, and the monks told him, "You are an imperfect human being." "This saying really hurt me," my friend confided.

True Buddhism is much harder than Westerners make it out to be. To some Westerners who don't really understand, Buddhism may seem like an easy alternative to Christianity. For them to say, "I'm more interested in Buddhism," is often their way of rejecting Christianity. But the fact is Buddhism is not the all-accepting path for anyone to follow. It prescribes a definite set of strict rules and conditions, much like the Biblical Old Testament. It proscribes a long list of immoral behavior. Buddhism shares much in common with the Old Testament and there are many bridges one can build between the two. We find power and freedom only when we come into Christ, who alone fulfilled every moral requirement God placed on humans.

The strict laws of Buddhism, like those of the Old Testament, leave one more conscious of one's imperfection. "I felt broken inside," my friend continued to tell me, "because in Buddhism we believe that if we become a monk, we can go to Heaven. But if I can't be a monk, then I will go to Hell. My friend tried to help me and told me to be a monk in another religion. 'Be a Brahman,' he said. But I thought Brahmanism doesn't promise anyone can go to Heaven."[8]

"So I said to myself, 'My life will not end up in Heaven. I will fall into Hell. And what will happen to my mother? She can wait for my younger brother to be a monk for her. But what about me? I will miss out on Heaven.'

"I thought often about this, 'I will not go to Heaven.' I worried about it and even became angry, 'This is unjust! How can I go to Heaven?' I even hated Buddhism. But I continued to act like a normal Buddhist and continued to *tam boon*.

"My friend became a monk for 3 months and after that he came out exactly the same as he was before. He went out clubbing, smoking, drinking, taking ecstasy drugs from Holland, sleeping around, and going for massages and prostitutes. Nothing had changed, and it seemed to me, nothing could ever change his inside. He even invited me to do drugs with him just like before.

"One night I had a dream. I saw a church with a cross on top of the steeple. This church was at the old school I used to attend. I stood on the grassy fields and looked up and saw the cross. At first I thought I was just thinking about my Christian school or my childhood. I woke up and immediately told my girlfriend about it, 'I dreamed about the cross on top of my old school. This cross was very high!' Quite naturally I forgot about this incident.

"One week later I dreamed another dream. I was standing in front of my school and I looked up at the cross again. I woke up and said to my girlfriend, 'Can you believe it? I had the same dream again! It's probably time I go back and visit my old school. I must be missing my old school. I'll take you there, but it's very far away, near the border of Laos.' This was the second time.

"Another week passed. I dreamed the same dream again. I saw the same cross. I stood at the same spot. I started feeling uneasy and bothered. 'What's going on?' I thought, 'Did I do something wrong in that place? Why do I have to go back there?'"

By this time my friend's girlfriend Mali wanted to add her side of the story, "That week after my exam, I met a friend on an ABAC university bus. I remembered that she once told me, 'Today I'm going to church because it's Christmas!' She never told me anything else, but I figured that she must be a Christian. So I told her about my boyfriend's dream. I was searching for the meaning of this dream. I asked her, 'What does this mean?' She had an answer I didn't like, 'God is calling you!'

"Mali was very anti-Christian," my friend told me, "because she thought that going to church meant you had to be a good person. Unless you were pure, you couldn't go to church. So I didn't understand why God would be calling us. We lived such sinful lives!

"But we decided that we will go to church of our own accord. We really were searching by this time. There must be something if you dream the same dream three times! So we went to church to get the meaning.

"That week the movie *The Passion* came out and we went to watch it. We were very curious. Who was this person who was beaten? Why was he beaten? We hardly understood the movie, especially when the adulteress was caught. We understood nothing, but we wanted to understand. We were really curious.

"So we arranged to meet Mali's friend at 9am because church started at 10am on 8 August 2004. It happened to be a Mother's Day service. My friend was a Children's Church teacher so she had to arrive early to arrange the children's performance. We woke up late and thought, 'It's too late. We don't have to go.' But Mali had really set her mind on going.

So we drove out not knowing exactly where the church was, except to go near a certain Department Store. We called our friend to ask how to drive there, and she said it was amazing that we had called, because she had forgotten her phone at home, and felt led to go back and get it. She told us, 'I'm doing a U turn right now. Where are you at?' It turned out we were at the same U turn, and her car was right in front of our car!

"We entered the church and really enjoyed all the things the children were doing for their mothers. I felt very warm inside. It was a feeling I had never known before. This was what I had wanted to do for my own mother! The pastor asked us to pray after her to receive Jesus into our hearts. She gave us a brand new Bible. Since we had just seen *The Passion of the Christ*, we really wanted to read the Bible. We finished the New Testament in a short time and we felt this was a lot of fun to read! Now we understood the life of Jesus.

"The second time we went back to church, we were asked to testify how we had come to this little church. I told the pastor about all my dreams. I dreamt about this school. The pastor was so surprised, 'I went to that school!' God was confirming His message to me! We felt a spiritual connection with her.

"In our fourth week of attending church, I started to doubt the Bible. I began to question, 'Who are these people – John the Baptist, Paul, and Herod? Are they real people? Or are they tricking me? I'm supposed to be a Buddhist!' Deep in doubt, I fell asleep. When I woke up, I turned on the news and on TV they reported that they had discovered a cave of John the Baptist. They said it was archaeological evidence that confirmed the Bible. It showed the place where John the Baptist ministered and even described how John the Baptist baptized sinners. I suddenly felt, 'There really is a God!'

"Then I dreamed for the last time. God gave me my last dream. I was no longer standing outside the church. This time I was standing inside. I looked up and I saw no more walls to block my way to God. I saw the paintings of scenes of the Bible on the walls. I felt a surpassing peace and comfort. I knew God had prepared everything for me. This is what my Christian life is like up till now."

The Polio Victim thought he had a chance to purify his own karma until he actually visited a monk and came face to face with the reality of Buddha's 227 commandments. Being told his inability to meet the physical requirements in 32 bodily parts and moral requirements of Buddha may have seemed like a cruel rejection, but it actually saved his life! The demands of the moral laws broke his pride. Honest self-awareness made him more humble and willing to hear God's solution for him.

In the next chapter, we will look at how Jesus would have dealt with such a man.

# 10

# HOW JESUS MADE HIMSELF KNOWN

Jesus knows the number of hair on your head. Jesus knows every sparrow flying through the air. I imagine it is probably difficult for Jesus to hold back all He knows! He knows what will save us. He knows how to fix every problem in our lives. But like a good doctor, He doesn't offer us a cure until He has given us a proper diagnosis of our disease.

The art of diagnosing the sinner's problem has been lost to the modern church. We insist rather on giving the solution, "Just trust in Jesus!" This baffles most listeners because they don't *feel* any personal need to trust in Jesus. They are not aware of the disease for which Jesus is the only cure. If we continue to bait the seeker with the promises of the Gospel, "You won't ever find true happiness and peace until you have Jesus," many seekers will simply think that's untrue. Many sinners are enjoying the life God gave them without acknowledging God. We may argue that their happiness is only temporary, while ours is eternal, but now we are no longer preaching the Gospel Jesus gave us.

Never did Jesus say, "I'm happier than you. That's why you ought to believe Me!" While happiness is one fruit of believing in Christ, happiness was never the central issue of the Gospel.

# What is?

The disease Jesus came to cure is sin. Sin is an epidemic that results in suffering, death, and eternal separation from a Loving and Holy God. Do people acknowledge that they are sinners? Not usually. That's why God wrote the Old Testament and sent the Holy Spirit – both of which can identify and measure this invisible virus. The purpose of God's Old Testament Laws is to help us realize the extent to which we are sick with sin. The Law prepares the sinner's heart for the Gospel. Without the Law, there would be no conviction of sin. Without conviction of sin, there would be no repentance. Without repentance, there could be no true conversion or faith in Christ.

James wrote, "You commit sin, and are convicted of the law as transgressors" (James 2:9). The Book of Romans is Paul's treatise on the Gospel. In it Paul wrote, "I would not have known sin except through the law. For I would not have known covetousness unless the law had said, 'You shall not covet'" (Romans 7:7), quoting the last of the Ten Commandments. "For by the law is the knowledge of sin" (Romans 3:20). J.B. Phillips translation puts it this way, "If there were no Law the question of sin would not arise...Now we find that the Law keeps slipping into the picture to point the vast extent of sin" (Romans 3:20, 5:20) Paul said Christians should explain the Law "so that sin through the commandment might become exceedingly sinful" (Romans 7:13).

It surprises many Christians that the Holy Spirit has been sent to confirm God's Law. The first ministry of the Holy Spirit is "He will convict the world of *sin*, and of righteousness, and of judgment" (John 16:8). Today preachers tend to talk about becoming righteous in Christ without talking about sin or judgment. Sin is objectively defined by God's Law and God's judgment will be based on His unchangeable Laws.

## HOW JESUS USED THE LAW LAWFULLY

Because there is so little teaching these days on sin and judgment, we forget that Jesus made constant reference to God's Holy Law in His proclamation of the Gospel. There is no better Gospel preacher than Jesus! There were three instances where seekers literally walked up to Jesus and said, "Tell me how I can get saved!" How did Jesus respond? In all three cases, Jesus said, "What does the Law say?" (Luke 10:26) and "If you want to enter into life, keep the commandments" (Matthew 19:16, Luke 18:20) and "Go, call your husband (referring to her breaking the seventh commandment against adultery)" (John 4:16).

Jesus constantly pointed to God's Law, but here was the twist. He did not point to God's Law as the *solution*, but as a diagnostic *test* of our malady.

The Biblical Jesus pointed to God's Law to reveal *why* we all need a Savior. The hypothetical, modern version of Jesus would have said something like this to a seeker, "You have a God-shaped void in your heart, in fact a Jesus-shaped void in your heart, and if you would just open up your heart and accept Me, you'll be filled with peace and happiness!" If you read the New Testament, you'll find that the historical Jesus and early apostles never said that. Yet this is what most Christians seem to do.

If a sinner were to ask the average churchgoer today, "What must I do to have eternal life?" he might reply something like this, "You want to be saved?! Before you change your mind...repeat this prayer after me: O God, I open up my heart to let Jesus to come into my life. Forgive

me of my sins. I'm now born again in Jesus' name. Amen."
The sinner walks away thinking, "That was easy," yet you
will rarely see them again in church or committed to the
things of God. You the Christian then wonder to yourself,
"But they prayed the salvation prayer! What happened? I just
don't understand." What is the problem?

Modern evangelism has strayed away from Biblical
evangelism. Modern evangelism no longer sees God's laws as
paving the way for the Gospel. Today Christians tend to see
God's law as synonymous with "legalism." Some react
strongly against God's law, "It's legalistic to talk about the
law. It's a relic of the Old Testament." But the Apostle John
said in the New Testament, **"For the law was given
through Moses** [first]**, but grace and truth came through
Jesus Christ** [second]" (John 1:17).

The way God evangelized the world was to give the law
*first*, then grace *second*. The law revealed the problem of the
human heart, then grace revealed the answer for the human
heart. If there was a better way to write the Bible or
communicate His message to earthlings, God would have
done it. The Bible is God's genius. The Old Testament paved
the way perfectly for the New Testament.

## BRIDGING BUDDHISM AND CHRISTIANITY

Because Christians have long neglected the value of the law
and condemned its use in evangelism, Christians have not
seen the value of the teachings of Buddha. **Just as Moses'
laws paved the way for the Jews to find Jesus, Buddha's
laws can pave the way for Buddhists to find freedom
from karma**[1].

So you don't want to distance yourself from the law, but
propel sinners to the law, awakening their conscience to the
dangers of living and dying as law-breakers. God gave the law
as a powerful weapon to waken careless men's souls. If you

look at the New Testament, and look at how they evangelized, you'll find they used the law.

**1 TIMOTHY 1:8-10**

**8 But we know that the law is good if one uses it lawfully**

How does one use the law lawfully? The next verses tell us.

**9 knowing this: that the law is NOT made FOR a righteous person, BUT FOR the LAWLESS and insubordinate, for the ungodly and for SINNERS, for the unholy and profane, for murderers of fathers and murderers of mothers, for manslayers,**

**10for fornicators, for sodomites, for kidnappers, for liars, for perjurers, and if there is any other thing that is contrary to sound doctrine,**

The law was *not* made for the born again person. In other words, I as a born again person do not wake up each morning and read the Ten Commandments to remind myself, "Today, I must not kill anyone. I must not lie. I must not steal." Because God's new nature has been implanted into my heart, by His Holy Spirit, I no longer walk by the law, but by the Spirit. So preaching the law to Christians will tend to condemn the Christian and bind him to legalism. This is an illegitimate use of God's law.

What then is the legitimate use of God's law? 1 Timothy 1:9 tells us, "Knowing this: that the law is NOT made FOR a righteous person, BUT FOR the lawless...the ungodly and for sinners..." That means it's perfectly legitimate to preach the law to sinners and grace to the saints. However, most preachers have done it the other way around! We give grace to the sinners and law to the saints!

What is the result? We tend to produce saints who feel condemned most of the time and sinners who have prayed the "sinner's prayer" without an ounce of repentance. There was no repentance because there was no conviction. There was no conviction because we never spoke the Scriptures that are intended to bring conviction – that is, the law. The Bible says the law came by Moses but grace came by Jesus. No one's ready for Grace until they have first been convicted by the Law.

That's God's order. That's the Biblical way. That's how to evangelize. We can't improve on it. Whether you are speaking to a Jew, Muslim, Buddhist, atheist, or nominal Christian, God's Law must precede God's Grace. Fortunately, in Buddhism, we have a strong ally in Buddha's moral commands. They are virtually the same laws as God's laws.

These are what we will take a look at in the next few chapters.

# 11

# THE FIVE COMMANDMENTS OF BUDDHA

Obviously the 227 commands of Buddha are quite complicated and very difficult for everyone to remember or follow. So the monks have brought it down to 5 rules for the commoner. These rules are really the Christian's friends, so I am encouraging every Christian to remember these 5 rules. They are called the *benja seen* in Pali[1] or *seen ha* in Thai. *Seen* means commandment; *benja* means five in Pali and *ha* means five in Thai[2]. The *seen ha* are the 5 minimum prohibitions for the common Buddhist to keep. If you call yourself a Buddhist, you have got to keep these 5 every day of your life.

I will give each prohibition in Pali first, then translate it into our language, just like a Buddhist would learn it. As you will notice, the *seen ha* appear quite similar to the second half of the Ten Commandments.

Number 1: *Bana tipa-ta veramani!* **Do not kill.**
Some people I meet like to boast, "I can keep that rule! I've never killed anybody!" But I am sorry that is not what Buddha meant. He meant you cannot kill a mosquito

while it's biting you. You cannot kill a cockroach while it's crawling on your food. You cannot kill a rat while it's going through your bedroom even if you have little babies to protect. You cannot kill any termite if it's eating your house down.

Now I know for a fact that Buddhist homeowners kill termites all the time. They wouldn't think twice about getting the spray bottle out and killing all those cockroaches. Technically speaking, a Buddhist can't even kill bacteria, and every time you take antibiotics, you kill not only bad bacteria, but probiotics (good bacteria) as well.

"Don't kill" also means you can't eat any meat, you must be a vegetarian. All the wonderful Asian dishes that we love to eat have a lot of beef, pork and chicken in them; well, we are breaking one of the *seen ha*. If we want to be a Buddhist, we must never kill anything.

According to the Thai Dictionary of Buddhism[3], the full meaning of this commandment is to abstain from killing, molesting, hurting any life, or injuring anyone[4].


Number 2: *Atin-na ta-na veramani!* **Do not steal**.
Again, some people like to claim, "I can do that. I never steal." "Really?" I reply, "I would like to come to your house and check what's in your music collection and computer! If you have ever copied a song you didn't purchase or ever watched a pirated movie, you are a thief. You are stealing something that does not belong to you. And you are breaking one of Buddha's top five commandments.

The Thai Dictionary of Buddhism says the full meaning of this prohibition is to abstain from taking something without permission, stealing, cheating, violating ownership and proprietary rights and damaging the property of others.[5]

Some people I talk to have arguments for why they steal. They think piracy or violating other people's intellectual property rights is not theft. That's like the driver who is caught speeding arguing with the police that the speed limit is unfair. That's called justifying your sins, and that's what sinners do. Don't make light of your own sins. When someone pickpockets you, steals your purse, or burglarizes your home, you will not feel happy if the robber justifies himself, "You are too rich, so I thought it was alright to steal from you." Excuses are no defense. God is looking at the heart.

Number 3: *Garmay sumitcha jara veramani!* **Do not commit sexual immorality.**

That includes sex before marriage (fornication), sex after marriage with someone besides your spouse (adultery), sex with a non-consenting person (rape), sex with a minor (paedophilia), sex with a person of the same gender (homosexuality), sex with animals (bestiality), and sexual fantasy (pornography) - all of these acts make a person sexually unclean.

In traditional Asian cultures, immorality includes any inappropriate contact, kiss or touch with a person who is guarding her purity or does not want the attention. Buddha said don't do it. You can't achieve nirvana, go to Heaven, or escape suffering if you violate this prohibition. The safest way to abide by this prohibition, monks and nuns have found, is to vow life-long celibacy, but even then many monks have fallen into pornography, flirting, or breaking of their vows.

Number 4: *Musa wa-ta veramani!* **Do not lie or speak any evil.**

Some people lie so often they forget they lie out of habit. Students lie to teachers when they plagiarize. Some immigrants lie to immigration officers about their legal and marital status. People lie to the Tax Office about how much money they make and how much tax they should pay. Many real estate agents lie to close a sale and make a profit.

God said it doesn't matter who you lie to, why you lie, or when you lie, if you lie, there's no room for you in Heaven. In Heaven, we are going to be safe and able to trust each other. We cannot trust a liar, so only people who always tell the truth will live in Heaven. Heaven is going to be wonderful.

We are never going to be afraid or suspicious of anyone in Heaven. Suppose 99% of the population in Heaven told the truth, but just 1% lied, it wouldn't be called Heaven anymore; it would soon become Hell! For those of us who want to be part of Heaven, God says, "I have prepared a place called Heaven for all of you. But no lying!" If we have lied, we need to have our karma paid in full (which is possible only by Someone who has never lied – Jesus Christ).

When Buddha commanded people not to speak evil, it also included cussing, cursing, gossiping, and any idle talk. Have you kept this rule perfectly? The Apostle James said: "For we all stumble in many things. If anyone does not stumble in word, he is a perfect man, able also to bridle the whole body...And the tongue is a fire, a world of iniquity. The tongue is so set among our members that it defiles the whole body, and sets on fire the course of nature; and it is set on fire by Hell." (James 3:2, 6)

The "course of nature" can also be translated the "wheel of nature" or the "cycle of destruction and disaster" (The Living Bible). Our tongue sins easily and sets in motion the "cycle of destruction" – the Bible and Buddha agree with each other on this point. The Bible is clear: verbal offences are like uncontrollable flames of Hell. Lying is hellish. If we have ever lied, we need to repent and trust in the One who has never lied – Jesus Christ.

Number 5: *Sura may-ra-ya majjapama tat-tana veramani!* **Do not use any addictive substance.**

That refers to alcohol, cigarettes, drugs, etc. A very strict Buddhist might even say that includes coffee and any other addictive substance. Buddha said if you want to escape suffering, you cannot allow your flesh to be addicted to any substance.

As we shall see, these laws are very helpful when Christians talk to Buddhists.

# WHAT WOULD JESUS SAY TO BUDDHISTS?

## HOW TO STOP A CONVERSATION

If you take the most popular approach to evangelism, you may walk up to a Buddhist and quote them John 3:16, "For God so loved the world that He gave His only begotten Son that whosoever believes in Him should not perish but have everlasting life." You hope your Buddhist friend gets it, and in case she doesn't, you add, "Jesus loves you."

How will the typical Buddhist respond? I've literally had hundreds of conversations with Buddhists around the world, and they nearly always say the same thing: "But I am a Buddhist." That ends most conversations.

In all sincerity, the Christian starts off telling the Buddhist, "God loves you." In all sincerity, the Buddhist replies, "But I am Buddhist." It's a conversation stopper. Now what do you say?

If you're going to be effective at building bridges with your Buddhist neighbor, you need to know what to say after someone says, "I am Buddhist."

Those who are not accustomed to the typical Buddhist

answer ("I am Buddhist") have come up with interesting replies. Here are some I personally have heard:

One person said, "I would relate my personal experiences with God." That's one way.

Another person said, "Buddhists are trying to be free from attachments – they want to have no attachment to life, money, or relationships." In my opinion, this is repeating something from a textbook. I don't think you'd find the average Buddhist thinking about attachment or detachment. She would more likely be grateful for some divine help in this life of uncertainty and suffering.

Another person said, "You are Buddhist? That's great! God loves Buddhists, too." Not bad. Most conversations would have stopped at, "I'm Buddhist." At least you broke through a dead end. You're on your way!

Part of my work has been to help prepare Christians to present the Gospel to Buddhists at home and abroad. Let me give you some secrets on how to have spiritual conversations with Buddhists. The more you understand their religious background, their day to day life, their desire to interact with friendly, pure, prayerful Christians, the more confidence you will have in conversing about spiritual matters freely.

## WHEN YOU DON'T KNOW WHAT TO SAY!

When Christians meet Buddhists, they should use the teachings of Buddha to start a conversation because it's familiar to the Buddhist ear. Every Buddhist should know and try to live by the 5 Commandments of Buddha (Thai: *seen ha*). You don't want to start with "God loves you" because that is unfamiliar to their ear. Sharing the Good News effectively is simply taking someone from the familiar to the unfamiliar. If you don't start with the familiar, you really have not shared Good News.

The five basic prohibitions are the minimum rules

Buddhists should keep. The *seen ha* are definitely the teaching that any common, average Buddhist will be able to understand. They may not know all the other stuff in our Western textbooks, but they know this – the *seen ha*. And most know that they are guilty of breaking them fairly regularly.

To show you how seriously Buddhists take the *seen ha*, I refer to a debate that you may not have heard, but raged in Thailand in 2007. As politicians were drafting a new Thai constitution, certain monks wanted Buddhism to be recognized in the constitution as the official state religion of Thailand. After much debate, the drafters voted on 29 June 2007 to omit Buddhism as a state religion, much to the chagrin of many protesters. The reason? While there were probably many – political, historical and spiritual – we are concerned mostly about the spiritual.

Some asked if Thailand were to become a Buddhist nation, would her people be willing to stop selling beer (which breaks the 5th commandments of Buddha)? They asked if Thailand was willing to stop the illicit sex trade and punish all adultery (which breaks the 3rd commandment of Buddha)? They asked if Thailand was willing to stop selling meat (which breaks the 1st commandment of Buddha)? And if Thais were not willing or could not keep the *seen ha*, what purpose would it serve to call Thailand 'Buddhist'?

When someone says to me, "I am Buddhist," I usually affirm, "That's great! Can you keep the 5 commandments of Buddha?" In nearly every instance, I will get a smile or a laugh. It's a cover-up laugh… a laugh of conviction. Buddhists will tend to brush the personal guilt aside and make the blame universal, "*Nobody* keeps the *seen ha*."

## WHAT WOULD JESUS SAY TO BUDDHISTS?

The five commandments of Buddha are nearly identical to the Ten Commandments of Moses. It would not be surprising if the Buddhist five were based on the original Mosaic Ten, since Moses was a thousand years older than Buddha and God's laws to Moses were revolutionary and would have been well known to all civilized people.

Jesus made great use of the Ten Commandments in evangelism. When a rich ruler asked Him, "Good Teacher, what shall I do to inherit eternal life?" Jesus quoted five of the Ten Commandments:

**Do not commit adultery** [commandment no. 7],
**Do not murder** [commandment no. 6],
**Do not steal** [commandment no. 8],
**Do not bear false witness** [commandment no. 9],
**Honour your father and your mother** [commandment no. 5] (Luke 18:18-20).

Why did Jesus quote the five commandments to the rich ruler? For the same reason I quote the five commandments to a Buddhist. To gauge his honesty. Why didn't Jesus simply tell the rich ruler to believe in Him? Couldn't Jesus have made it easier for him to get saved by saying, as many Christians do, "God loves you. Jesus loves you. Just believe in Jesus and you'll be fine"?

Jesus didn't do that because He did not "come to call the righteous, but sinners, to repentance" (Luke 5:32, 15:7). This rich ruler was self-righteous. He would not admit that he was a sinner. His standard of "good" was much lower than God's. So to expose the rich ruler's true sinful condition and his need for forgiveness from God, Jesus quoted five of the holy commandments the man had broken.

But what was the ruler's reply? "I've kept all these from my youth"!

In all honesty, what would you say was the possibility of a proud, rich, young man having never lied, stolen or engaged in any form of sexual impurity? Nil?

In Matthew's account, Jesus added on top of the five commandments the Great Commandment, "AND, you shall love your neighbor as yourself" (Matthew 19:19). No one, other than Jesus, has ever loved everybody else as himself. That last commandment should have convicted the rich ruler, but he still had the impression that he was a basically good person. Finally, because Jesus "loved him" (Mark 10:21), He gave him one more commandment to expose the ruler's love for sin. Jesus told him to sell all that he had and follow Him. But he loved money too much to leave it.

This verse has been one of the most misunderstood verses in the Gospel. Some have wondered, "If I am a Christian, must I sell all that I own to follow Jesus?" I have met Christian sects who practice this. Other Christians have interpreted Jesus' statement to mean that He is against the rich and poverty is holy. This is lifting Jesus' statement out of context. Jesus was not addressing Christians or teaching on discipleship. Jesus was talking to a proud, self-righteous sinner and He was evangelizing him! Unless a Christian is proud and self-righteous (in which case I wonder how he is Christian), he should have no problem working, earning money, giving, saving, investing, blessing the poor, all as the Bible commands him to in many places.

The purpose of Jesus' command for this rich man to give up all earthly possessions was evangelistic. It was to expose his true love for money above his love for God. His refusal to let go of money and to follow Jesus proved he broke the first, second and tenth commandments of God (to love God means to put Him first before money; to not worship any idol including the idol of money; to not covet or be greedy for money). The rich man went away "very sorrowful", and this was a better outcome than continuing in his pride and self-righteousness.

In the book of Acts, we find the record of a man who sold all he had, donated to the church and followed Jesus (Acts 4:36-37). Some believe this humbled man Barnabas was the same rich man who met Jesus; he apparently got convicted and saved later after his first encounter with Jesus. That's the power God's moral law has on sinners!

In a similar vein, Buddha taught people to keep at least 5 moral commandments. The dedicated monk must keep 227. When someone says to me, "You are Christian, but I am Buddhist," I turn what is ordinarily a conversation stopper into a spiritual springboard. Following Jesus' example above, I ask, "Can you keep the 5 commandments of Buddha?"

13

# THE KOREAN BUDDHIST

I remember talking to a Korean Buddhist who was riding in the same cable car as my wife and I. Because South Korea has become a very Christian country[1], I thought to myself, "He is Korean, he's probably already Christian." When I asked him about it he said, "No, I'm not Christian," and stayed silent. I thought, "Probably a lot of Christians have tried to witness to him." So I politely asked, "What do *you* believe?"

Rather than attacking people's religions or overloading them with Christianity, I believe Christians need to learn to ask better questions. He replied, "I am Buddhist!" He said it not expecting any more conversation with this Christian stranger. But I loved the fact that he gave me an open door. I excitedly replied, "Really? You are Buddhist? That's great! I was Buddhist, too! I came from the world's largest Buddhist country. Do you know Thailand? Thailand is a very Buddhist country!" He seemed to relax. Perhaps he was thinking, "We have something in common."

I continued, "So are you able to keep the commandments of Buddha?"

Now he's sweating a little bit. I could almost see him

searching his head, "I ought to know the commandments! Somebody once taught me the commandments of Buddha."

Don't be surprised by Buddhists who can't remember their own commandments. It is not so different from Westerners who went to Catholic school or grew up as a nominal Christian; most I meet can't tell you the Ten Commandments by heart either.

I asked him a second time, "There are just five commandments of Buddha. Can you remember any of the five?"

He said, "Wait a minute, I can remember.... Number one, don't kill."

I said, "Do you keep that?"

He said, "Yeah, I never kill anybody."

I followed up to make sure he's honest, "Do you eat bulgogi[2]?"

He said, "Oh, yeah, every Korean eats bulgogi."

I said, "Isn't that killing? What's another commandment you can remember?"

He thought about it for a while. He was actually pretty good because given enough time he could remember two more, and the rest he forgot.

So I went over each commandment one by one, "Do you ever steal?"

He happily said, "No!"

But his happiness was short-lived when I followed up, "Do you mean you have never downloaded music from the internet that you shouldn't have or listened to an illegal copy of a CD or watched a pirated DVD?"

He seemed surprised at himself, "Oh...!" He gave a guilt-covering smile.

I gently reminded him, "That's stealing. Buddha also said, Never lie. Have you ever lied?" He nodded.

"Do not commit adultery, and that would include all sexual impurity."

"Lastly, do not drink or take an intoxicating drug."

Within five minutes of a very friendly conversation, the conviction of the Holy Spirit came. Out of his own mouth, the young man said, "I'm not a very good Buddhist." He recognized himself as a sinner deserving suffering.

I asked him, "If you were to die today and be judged for how you have lived your life before God, should you be punished or rewarded?" He believed, as both Jesus and Buddha taught, that his sins deserved to be punished. If there is any Justice in the universe, sin must be paid for by suffering and death. The Bible warns, "The soul that sins, it shall die" (Ezekiel 18:4).

When this man saw that he was spiritually sick, only then could I introduce him to the Great Physician. When he saw he was a sinner, only then could I introduce him to the Loving Savior. Otherwise he would have despised what I had to say about Jesus. He had previously believed he was a perfectly good Buddhist, until he was confronted with the reality that he could not follow his own religion very well. God's commands are not merely 5, but 10 from Mount Sinai, and 613 if you count them all up in the Old Testament. When people see their spiritual problem, only then will they seek the spiritual solution.

## WHAT DOES THIS KEY OPEN?

If you want to help someone, never give them the answer without first clearly defining the problem. That's the trouble with modern Christian methods of evangelism. It's as if Christians are going around handing out keys to people, proclaiming "Jesus died for you. Jesus loves you," but the Buddhist looks at this key and wonders, "What does this key do? What does this open?"

Suppose for a minute I have a key that opens a vault full of solid gold. Suppose further that the person I'm addressing is in great debt. This key that I hold could be the answer to his financial troubles. But unless I first reveal to him the state of his financial condition, he may very well throw away the key! So I might remind him, "You've got credit card debt, you've been laid off, you have bills up to your ears, and what you need is a financial breakthrough, right? Well this key will open a safe that has some gold in it and I'm giving it to you. You could exchange this gold for money to pay off your debt and live off the rest. Here's the key!"[3]

What would be the reaction of this man? Anger? Disgust? Or deepest appreciation? If he is sensible he will say, "Wow, I don't deserve this. I messed up my own finances. I made some bad financial decisions. Are you sure?"

"It's okay," I reassure him, "I give you the key. It's a free gift."

Because his problem was clearly defined, the solution I offered was accepted with heartfelt gratitude.

Christians really do hold a key to a vault full of solid gold. It's imperishable, eternal wealth in Christ! Yet some people have taken the key and rejected it because they never knew what sort of trouble they were in. No Christian dared to tell them the problem of sin and its subsequent suffering. A great key was tossed aside. Jesus would say that Christians have been casting pearls to swine and giving what is holy to dogs (Matthew 7:6). Dogs and pigs don't appreciate pearls. They don't know the value of it.

If you share the Gospel Biblically by defining man's problem first, more people will appreciate the pearl (the answer) you're offering them. But if you preach it poorly, skipping the important part of the moral law, most people will feel offended. Their attitude will be, "What's the point of your giving this to me? I don't need Jesus! I don't think I've sinned. I'm a good person. I haven't killed anybody. Why don't you leave me alone and go talk to someone who needs a religious crutch!" Can you see why they might feel that way?

When I went through the 5 commandments of Buddha, which form a partial list of God's holy commandments in the Bible, conviction came upon this Korean man, right there in the cable car, a thousand feet up in the air. He couldn't go anywhere and he admitted, "I'm not a very good Buddhist." I just let that truth sink in. I didn't try to comfort him straight away. I just wanted him to know: we all must come to that self-realization that despite our religious fronts, we are far from perfect and fall short of the glory of God (Romans 3:23).

I did not say that I was different from him. In fact, we're all the same... we're all bad Buddhists! We are all incapable of keeping the laws of Buddha, just as the Jews were incapable of keeping the laws of Moses, just as Christians are incapable of keeping the laws of Jesus.

C hristians should have it easiest as Jesus gave us only two laws: Love God with everything we've got (in other words, always put God first in everything we do); and love our neighbors as much as we love ourselves (Matthew 22:37-40). How many of us meet those standards? Love our neighbor? Let's start with loving our spouses! How many of us go home and always treat our wives or husbands as we would like to be treated? After a long day at work, we would like to kick back, relax, and do nothing, right? So if we truly love our wives as ourselves, we would say, "Honey, here's the couch and the remote control, sit right here while I go do the laundry, wash the dishes, and prepare us a nice meal to eat." That is "loving your neighbor as yourself." Whatever your body wants, do that for your neighbors! Most of us fail to do that for our closest loved ones! Husbands, wives, parents, children, friends, we all put our needs and wants above others' desires and often above God's desires. We fail to love God and love our neighbors. If love is the standard to get to Heaven, and Jesus said it is, then all of us are already disqualified to be in Heaven.

When we come to that realization, it's a great day! Now we are closer to salvation than ever before. We are closest to Heaven when we realize **it's hard to be good without God**. Then we are willing to say, "Lord, show me the way. I cannot save myself. I need Your help! Come into my heart right now, forgive my sins, wash me clean through Jesus' Blood, and make me as Your child." That's what it takes to become a Christian. Repent and believe Jesus. Ask Jesus for His help, He is waiting to save you!

# THE TEN KARMAS

It shocks most Westerners to learn that Buddha taught and clearly defined sin. In fact Buddha taught there are "10 ways of karma"[1] or "10 ways of death that will cause a human to go to Hell".[2] Did you read that correctly? Yes, you did. Buddha said if you break any one of these laws you will go straight to Hell. How come in Western classes on Buddhism, we never hear the words sin, punishment or Hell taught? Because it sounds too much like what the Western enthusiasts are trying to reject - Christianity.

Buddha said this: there are 10 ways to go to Hell. These 10 ways of death are similar to what a Catholic may call the 7 deadly sins. In reality, any sin is deadly and will take you to Hell, but the 7 deadly sins are especially repugnant. Likewise any karma is bad for you but if you've got one of these 10 karmas, you've definitely got no hope! Buddha said if one is guilty of one sin, one is guilty of them all. Doesn't that sound like a verse in the Bible?

**JAMES 2:10**

**10 For whoever shall keep the whole law, and yet stumble in one point, he is guilty of all.**

How many laws do you have to break to be a law-breaker?

Just one. How many lies do you have to tell to be a liar? Just one. How many sins do you have to commit to be a sinner? Just one. Anyone who fails one law fails the entire law.

Buddha categorized these 10 laws into 3 groups:

Physical sins (Thai: *gaya-gum*)

Verbal sins (Thai: *wajee-gum*)

Mental sins (Thai: *mano-gum*).

Buddha amplified each category further.

**There are 3 kinds of *gaya-gum* or physical sins:**

Number 1: killing. Buddha didn't just mean killing a human being, he meant killing any life. You eat pork? You committed it. You're not a vegetarian? You're done for. You have *gaya-gum*, and you're going straight to Hell. (This is according to Buddha, not according to Jesus. God saved several murderers, changed them and used them for His glory, including Moses and Paul.)

Number 2: stealing. It doesn't matter the value of what you steal, whether it's a paper clip from the office or a song off the Internet. If you steal you have *gaya-gum*.

Number 3: committing adultery.

**There are 4 kinds of *wajee-gum* or verbal sins:**

Number 1: idle talk. Listen to the definition of this sin according to the Thai dictionary: talking nonsense, talking without a point, talking without knowing when to stop. If you do any of these you're going straight to Hell, according to Buddha.

Number 2: lying is a *wajee-gum*.

Number 3: insulting is a *wajee-gum*.

Number 4: cussing or speaking any rude words is a *wajee-gum*.

**There are 3 kinds of *mano-gum* or mental sins:**

Number 1: ill will. In other words, wishing harm on others, not letting go of hurt and holding onto grudges. If you have one of those you have *mano-gum*, you're not going to make it after you die.

Number 2: self-deception. Buddha was very specific in defining this disease of the human heart: "believing wrong things are right" and "trying to turn wrong things to appear right." That's self-deception. Self-deceived people will go where other self-deceived people are, Hell. Heaven is a place of truth only.

Number 3: greed. The Bible calls this "coveting". Many of us look at the word greed and think we're free from it, but let me give you another word for greed: a competitive or comparative spirit. Why do we compare ourselves with others? Whenever we fall into the temptation of comparing ourselves, feeling short-changed or cheated, we are succumbing to a destructive mental attitude. Greed! "How come the boss noticed her and not me? How come this younger person is making more money or driving a better car than I am? Why did she get the promotion when she hasn't even been working as long or as hard as I have? Why do they have this happy marriage and I'm always in the wrong relationship?" All these thoughts come from jealousy and greed. We are not in a race against other people. God gave each of us our own race and we don't get rewarded for beating others, but for being faithful with what we've got. You are in your own race, so run it well! If we have a competitive or comparative spirit, greed grows inside. Buddha said greed is one of the karmas that will definitely take you to Hell, so Buddhism is much harder than the ordinary Westerner thinks it is. It is not about world peace and harmony with nature and it's not so easy that you can do whatever you want. That is not the teaching of Buddhism.

Later in the chapter *King Asoka & the Python* we will see an illustration of a *mano-gum*. But first we will look at the Buddhist and Christian concepts of Hell.

# 15

# IS THERE A HELL?

Apopular belief is that since Buddhism teaches reincarnation, Buddhists do not believe in Hell. On the contrary, Buddhists have a very vivid idea of Hell. They say sinners will face demons[1] who will command them to "fall into a red hot copper wok"[2] and "climb a spiked cotton tree"[3]. In the *Tripitaka*[4], Buddha talked about both Heaven and Hell. Like Jesus, Buddha taught more about Hell than Heaven!

Buddha pointed out that people who have karma will go to one of the 8 levels or pits[5] of Hell, each representing a greater level of heat and torment. Whoever commits one of the 10 karmas, or breaks the 5 moral precepts (Thai: *seen ha*), will die and fall into Hell.

**1st pit of Hell:** *Sancheewa Narok* (narok means Hell)

For those who break the 1st basic moral law (*seen*). For those who kill animals, ants, mosquitos, other humans or self.

**2nd pit of Hell:** *Galasutta Narok*

For those who break the 2nd basic moral law. For those who like to cheat and steal.

**3rd pit of Hell:** *Sangkata Narok*

For those who break the 3$^{rd}$ basic moral law. For those who like to engage in sexual immorality, pornography, adultery, homosexuality, etc.

**4$^{th}$ pit of Hell:** *Roruwa Narok*

For those who break the 4$^{th}$ basic moral law. For those who like to lie, cuss, curse, tell vulgar jokes, talk non-stop or talk too much.

**5$^{th}$ pit of Hell:** *Maha-roruwa Narok*

For those who break the 5$^{th}$ basic moral law. For those who like to drink alcohol or use drugs.

**6$^{th}$ pit of Hell:** *Dapana Narok*

For anyone who likes to indulge in vice (*abayamuk*), which commonly refers to all forms of gambling including cards, betting, horseracing, slot machines, and going to casinos. Many Buddhists like to justify their sin and convince themselves that they can gamble because Buddha never said anything about gambling in the 5 moral precepts (*seen ha*). But Buddha said that gambling will lead you to the 6$^{th}$ lowest pit, worse than the first 5 pits reserved for those who break each of the *seen ha*!

*Abayamuk* is not one single sin, but a category of sins. One list shows that there are 4 *abayamuk's*, another list shows 6. A person who is guilty of *abayamuk* is called a *nakleng*, that is, someone who is unafraid and unashamed to sin, and often challenges others to duals, binge drinking, gambling, and other vices.

The 4 *abayamuk's* are: 1) *nakleng pooying* – womanizing, 2) *nakleng sura* – binge drinking and challenging others to drink, 3) *nakleng gan panan* – gambling as a profession, 4) keeping company with evil people.

The 6 *abayamuk's* are: 1) drinking, 2) going out at night (in the old days, there were very few places to go to, so going out at night equated to being up to no good), 3) loving entertainment, 4) gambling, 5) keeping company with evil people, 6) being too lazy to go to work. All 6 vices actually can be summarized as the typical lifestyle of the unemployed. Today many people who can work but live on government dole would be considered guilty of *abayamuk* by Buddha. Being useful is a virtue in Buddhism. Being unproductive is a great vice deserving of Hell.

**7th pit of Hell:** *Maha-dapana Narok*

For those who break all 5 moral precepts (*seen ha*). That is, they not only lie, but they also sleep around, steal, kill, and drink alcohol. It would be no exaggeration to say nearly every Buddhist alive would qualify.

**8th pit of Hell:** *Away-jee Narok*

The most famous level of Hell, referred to in popular phrases, threats, and traditional songs; as in, "You shouldn't do that! You will go to *Narok Away-jee!*"[6] For those who kill parents, monks, or Buddhas. For those who cause division in the religious community (or church splits). Some pastors would be glad for this one! Even if you do it once, according to Buddha, you must go to the worst Hell *Narok Away-jee*.

The lesson is, if we believe Buddha or Jesus, it's really easy to go to Hell! Buddha said the number of those who go to Heaven are like the horns of a cow, but the number of those who go to Hell are like the hairs of a cow's hide. You can ask a Buddhist, "Which is less, the number of horns or hairs?"[7] If they say the horns are fewer, then you can ask, "How many local people do you know who are following Jesus?" He will say not very many. (In Thailand it is only 1%.) We can all see it is a tragic few indeed! The horns are fewer than the hair.

Jesus taught us, "Wide is the gate and broad is the way that leads to destruction, and there are MANY who go in by it. Because narrow is the gate and difficult is the way which leads to life, and there are FEW who find it." What can prevent our being part of the masses who will carelessly go to Hell? Jesus continued in the next verse, "Beware of FALSE PROPHETS, who come to you in sheep's clothing, but inwardly they are ravenous wolves" (Matthew 7:13-15). Those who preach there is no Hell yet call themselves Buddhist or Christian look like sheep on the outside, but Jesus warned they are ravenous wolves on the inside. They are false prophets.

False prophets want us to believe that "Hell is an old religious concept invented to scare people into obedience, but we are too modern to believe such things now!" Is this really true? Science has shown that the Biblical description of Hell is startlingly accurate. The Bible says Hell is under the earth.[8] Under the earth is not Atlas as the Greeks claimed, or a Turtle as the American Indians claimed, or elephants as the Hindu Vedas claim, but layers of heat increasing in intensity. The earth's temperature rises 1°F for every 60ft in depth. The estimated temperature of the earth's core is 6650°C. The element sulphur (Biblical *brimstone*) has been discovered as a component of the earth's mantle. It would suffocate every breath you would try to take. There are things we still don't understand going on down there.

The Bible is vivid and scientific about its description of Hell. There will no longer be any water to drink[9] (can you imagine no relief from thirst forever?), nor fresh air to breathe[10] (can you imagine not being able to breathe properly for eternity?), nor sunlight to see[11] (can you imagine total darkness?), nor opportunity to rest[12] (can you imagine needing to sleep but never sleeping again for eternity?), nor a friend to talk to[13] (can you imagine no more conversation with anyone?), nor any sense of purpose whatsoever (can you imagine absolutely no one caring about you? If you think nobody cares about you now, try missing a couple of mortgage payments!). None of these good things we enjoy on earth will be there because water, air, sun, rest, work and friends are all blessings of God, and Hell is devoid of all God's blessings.

What will be there? Everything evil we have ever

encountered. Worms, maggots, snakes, beasts and terrible monstrosities[14]... all of which hate *you*[15], because they hate God[16], and you are created in God's image and likeness. They will torment you forever but you will never die. In fact, you will have an heightened sense of awareness. Can you imagine? On earth, one sting or bite can kill you. In Hell, you can be stung, bitten, beaten and torn apart without ever dying.

You may say, "I can't believe a loving God would create such a place called Hell." I understand. Suppose you were God, what would you do? Would *you* allow liars into Heaven? Would *you* allow rapists into Heaven? Both Buddha and Jesus have thought this through and concluded that sinners must go to Hell, morally to be punished and practically to be quarantined from the rest of Heaven's society. How else can God deliver justice to the victims and protect the innocent from becoming future victims? What makes Hell so bad is not God. It is precisely the opposite – His absence! He only needs to put all sinners together, both angelic and adamic, and they will make a Hell beyond imagination.

In medical science there is a condition called "**anesthesia awareness**," in which a patient undergoing surgery can feel everything happening to him, but he cannot communicate to anyone. One Baptist pastor who felt 15 minutes of his insides being operated on was so traumatized that he committed suicide. That was only 15 minutes! Hell will not be 15 minutes of pain, but an eternity. Hell is a prison which you can never escape.

You may say, "Hell is on earth." This is only partially true, because there is still a lot of good on earth. Thank God we get a probationary period on earth where we get to see a little bit of Heaven and a little bit of Hell, and get to choose which one we want for eternity. I'm sure those who have experienced "anesthesia awareness" or seen the human barbarity enacted in war think they have had a taste of Hell.

But on earth, surgery ends and wars eventually stop. In Hell, there is no God to stop them. Hell is the abode of every evil person and evil being. I know many sick people wish they were dead, because they expect their pain will end. But unless they are saved, what will they wake up to after death? Sadly, more of the same, only in greater intensity, lasting not weeks nor months, but forever. What a horrible realization that must be for those who die outside of faith in the Lord.

No one has to go to Hell. God does not want any of us to go there. It's not God sending people to Hell. It's the devil who has a legal right to snatch every sinner as his own possession. *"Do you not know that TO WHOM you present yourselves slaves to OBEY, you are THAT ONE's slaves whom you obey…?"* (Romans 6:16). It's not God overseeing these torments, but the devil whom we worship when we ignore our sinful living and refuse every opportunity to repent and believe in Jesus. Hell is real.

The foremost thought in my heart when I'm witnessing to Buddhists is that no loss will occur even if the Bible proves to be wrong; in fact, we will have enjoyed a good Christian life. But no price can pay for our loss if the Bible is right, and we chose to live in sin and reject God. If there is one chance in a million that Jesus might be right, and we might end up in that awful place, we owe it to ourselves to investigate who Jesus really is before we die!

## QUESTION & ANSWER

W ill I go to Hell just because I don't believe in Jesus?

No. People go to Hell because they are sinners. You will die and go to Hell only if you remain a sinner.

The person who sins is a sinner. *"The soul that sins, it shall die"* (Ezekiel 18:4). Jesus said, *"Therefore I said to you that you will DIE IN YOUR SINS, for you will DIE IN YOUR SINS unless you believe that I am he"* (John 8:24 RSV). Sinners die because of their sins. Refusing to believe in Jesus is not the reason they die.

Some preachers have popularized the idea that the only sin that will condemn a person to Hell is the "sin of not believing Jesus". Consequently many Christians have told sinners that they will go to Hell for not believing in Jesus. This is not only unscriptural, it's offensive. It makes people mad, "Are you saying I'm going to Hell because I'm not a Christian?" It doesn't make any sense to the average person.

The New Testament says, *"...All liars will have their part in the Lake of Fire"* (Revelation 21:8). John said, *"Whoever hates his brother is a murderer, and you know that no murderer has eternal life..."* (1 John 3:15). Paul said, *"Do not be deceived. Neither fornicators, nor idolaters, nor adulterers, nor homosexuals, nor sodomites, nor thieves, nor covetous, nor drunkards, nor revilers, nor extortioners will inherit the kingdom of God"* (1 Corinthians 6:10).

Clearly the New Testament teaches that people will go to Hell for various sins they are guilty of:

for lying [breaking the 9th commandment],

for hating [breaking the 6th commandment],

for fornicating [having sex with someone's future husband or wife, breaking the 7th commandment],

for worshipping idols [breaking the 2nd commandment],

for thieving [breaking the 8th commandment],

for coveting [breaking the 10th commandment],

for reviling [slandering or blaspheming, breaking the 3rd

commandment],

for extorting [misusing authority to get money, breaking the 8th and 10th commandments].

From where does the idea come that sinners go to Hell for not believing in Jesus? My own study points to some 18th-19th century commentaries popular among pastors (I'd rather not name them because that would not be walking in love). These popular commentators focus on only one Scripture to create this doctrine: "And when He [the Holy Spirit] has come, He will convict the world of sin, and of righteousness, and of judgment: of sin, because they do not believe in Me" (John 16:8-9).

It is noted that the word "sin" is in the singular, implying there is only one sin that condemns the soul. This interpretation ignores a myriad of other Scriptures, four of which we have just quoted. And the word sin is in the singular in many other places, referring to the category of "sin", and no point is made of it. For instance, "we [Christians] should no longer be slaves to sin" (Romans 6:6). Does this refer to the single sin of unbelief? Or was Paul referring to all sins of the flesh which we Christians should avoid, as the context suggests?

Jesus said the Holy Spirit will convict the world of sin, *because they do not believe in Me.* This could mean that the only sin the Holy Spirit will convict us of is the sin of unbelief. Or this could simply mean the Holy Spirit's ministry is to show the world what sin is and to convince the world that they are sinners; and until they receive Jesus, they will remain sinners who need to be convicted of their sinful state. This interpretation not only agrees with the rest of Scripture, it makes sense to the sinner!

The day I got saved, I was not convicted of my unbelief in Jesus Christ. No! I did not have any personal relationship with Jesus Christ yet. I was convicted by my own sins, too long and too embarrassing a list to tell anyone. The Holy

Spirit revealed to my heart my true moral weakness, duplicity, and responsibility in hurting others' lives, for which I knew I deserved Hell.

Only after being saved and developing a personal relationship with Jesus did I realize that disbelieving Him is a great sin. He is so good, He loves me so much, His Word is always true, why should I ever doubt Him?

The modern method of evangelism tends to ignore the heavy price of sin, so sinners are confused about why a loving God would send them to Hell. They think they're not really that bad. A loving and pure God knows the truth about each sinner, and will protect everyone in Heaven from a liar, a thief, a fornicator, a murderer, etc. He has to!

Buddha was not shy about preaching his 5, 8, 227, or even 311 commandments. Jesus, John and Paul were not shy about preaching God's Ten Commandments. The problem of not being able to keep the law drives people to the solution provided at Calvary. "Wherefore the law was our schoolmaster to bring us unto Christ, that we might be justified by faith" (Galatians 3:24).

People do not go to Hell because they are not Christian. People go to Hell because they are sinners. Refusing to believe in Jesus will not take you to Hell, but believing in Jesus is the only way to get you out of Hell. How can we escape our just sentence? By repenting and accepting Jesus' payment for our many sins.

# 16

## REINCARNATION

I f Buddha so clearly taught on Hell, what place does the doctrine of reincarnation have? Before we answer that (and we will dedicate several chapters towards this crucial question), let's understand a bit about reincarnation.

A growing minority of people in the West (one fifth of Americans[1]) say they believe in reincarnation. While this seems irksome to some Christian ministers, I believe this popular concept of Buddhism paves the way to Christianity! This is one of the best teachings of Buddha! I think it's the Christian's best friend! I wish everyone understood this because it's so easy to lead someone to Christ who truly understands *why* Buddha taught reincarnation.

Let me pose this simple question: Why should anyone have to be reincarnated? The short answer is, "It's what Buddha taught," but that doesn't answer *why* Buddha taught it. Why did he say people would have to come back?

Let's go over the basics. Buddhists believe that life is suffering and, much like anybody else, complain about their health, boss, salary, politicians, co-workers, spouse, and in-laws. No Buddhist *really* wants to be reincarnated. The Buddhist ideal is that each person lives a good life without sinning, accumulates lots of merits, and gets out of this wheel of suffering.[2]

Why did Buddha teach that most people will not attain this ideal, but have to be reincarnated instead? Because we still have sin or karma[3]. **We suffer in life because of our karma.** Every Buddhist knows that. This was the first teaching of Buddha – there is suffering. Buddha was wise. Why, Buddha, is there suffering? Buddha said because of your karma. That was Buddha's second teaching. Buddha was right! How can we escape from karma? Buddha's next answer leads us to reincarnation.

What reincarnation teaches is that our sin is so bad, we're going to have to pay for it all throughout this life, but when we're dead, it's not over. It's not enough. We still have to come back and pay for it again! And when we're born in the next life, we still will not have paid for it all, in fact we may have accumulated some more karma, so we will have to come back again and pay for it again. We will keep on paying and paying and paying because one life is not enough to pay for all our sins – that's how sinful sin is.

This belief is a great friend to evangelism! It brings such conviction to a person when they understand what their own religion teaches. You are in an absolutely hopeless and vicious cycle, according to Buddha himself. Isn't that powerful?

Yet many Christians, missionaries and pastors in Buddhist countries do not know that Buddha taught this because they tend to read Christian books by Western authors. The few who know it do not emphasize these similarities between Buddhism and Christianity. I met one pastor who was a Buddhist monk for many years before he became a Pentecostal Pastor. He used to use these similarities to build bridges with Buddhists, but now his stance is less friendly. It is as if he has been a Christian and a pastor for so long that all he can say about Buddhism is, "I hate it. It's evil. It's bad."

I believe he wins many people to the Lord using the traditional Western way, because God's Word is powerful. Whenever anyone speaks God's Word, it will produce results. So it's okay if some Christians don't want to build bridges. Everybody has different techniques and this is only one way. I am just equipping you with an extra tool in your cross cultural toolbox. If you tuck it away in your heart, it may help you understand the next Buddhist you're talking to.

## WHO HAS ESCAPED REINCARNATION?

Most Buddhists would say we don't know who has done it since Buddha. Buddha originally had 5 disciples; the 5 disciples then went out and taught what they learned from Buddha. Tradition would accept that these 5 actually broke the cycle and went to Nirvana.[4] But beyond the 5, we have little idea who else may have been able to do it.

Keeping all 227 commandments of Buddha perfectly is an impossible standard, which is what makes them so good! They keep people honest about who they really are – sinners. They act much like the Mosaic Law, an impossible standard that showed God's holiness and taught the Jews that they could never become righteous on their own efforts apart from God.

The Jewish rabbis, of course, found ways to justify their moral failures, rather than humbly repent and seek the blood atonement of the Savior. Some Buddhists also do the same. They know that if they kill a chicken, they will have to be reborn as a chicken that will also get killed. Rather than repenting and believing in the cleansing blood of the Savior, many Buddhists will justify their sinful action. Before they kill the chicken, they will talk to the chicken, "I am going to help you reincarnate faster, OK? So please forgive me for killing you." This is not what Buddha or Jesus taught. They did not want us to find moral loopholes. God wants us to know, we can never become righteous apart from Him. He, through Jesus Christ, is willing to impart righteousness to us.

The joy of Buddhist Heaven is that when you're gone, you're not coming back. You cease to be conscious. The joy of Christian Heaven is that we will continue to live in the most exciting relationship with a Good God! All the joys we felt in life will pale in comparison to the joys of being united with the Creator of Joy and Love and every good thing we've ever encountered on earth!

QUESTIONS & ANSWERS

Do you see any negatives about the belief in reincarnation?

As I said before, I believe Christians should not feel threatened by anyone's belief in reincarnation. Why do Buddhists believe we should come back again and again? Because we are sinners! All our sins must be paid for and it's not enough to suffer one lifetime. Reincarnation illustrates the impossibility of paying for sins in one life. Indeed, sins can never be erased by one's good deeds. The Good News becomes good news to the Buddhist when she realizes that Jesus is the only Sinless Person who broke the cycle of suffering, and He can break the cycle of suffering in our lives, too.

But I do not believe in reincarnation. First and foremost, the Bible tells me plainly that "it is appointed unto men ONCE to DIE, but after this the judgment" (Heb 9:27).

Secondly, reincarnation contradicts all observable evidence. The belief is that if we do good, we get to come back as a higher life form; but if we do bad, we must come back as a lower life form and work our way up again. If this were true, why don't we see well-behaved mosquitoes, flies, or cockroaches? After all, the mosquito that bit me could be my uncle trying to get promoted to a higher life form. All animals I have ever seen act instinctively and without concern for morals. This contradicts reincarnation.

Thirdly, as Scott Noble so adroitly writes, if reincarnation is real: "Why isn't it obvious among the billions of people in the world, regardless of cultural background? Why can't babies speak the language of their 'former life'…" For those who claim they do remember their past lives, Nobel asks, "Why does a person need to be under hypnosis…or be in an altered state of consciousness during meditation, in order to have such 'memories'?"[5] We know that testimonies of those who were previously hypnotized are inadmissible as evidence in court. Psychologists call it "false memory syndrome". Some Christians would call it "demon possession".

Fourthly, what many Westerners don't realize is that most believers in reincarnation are **racist**. Reincarnation originated from Hinduism, which is a religion based on a caste system. Hindus believe that being born with dark skin is the result of bad karma, but being born with white skin is a sign of good karma. The word "Aryan" which Nazis used to refer to a "master race" actually comes from a Sanskrit word meaning "noble". (As in *arya sat yani* in Sanskrit or *ariya sat si* in Thai, meaning the "four noble truths".) Adolf Hitler developed his racist plans from two anti-Christian sources: evolution and Hinduism. Nearly all Hindus and Buddhists who believe in reincarnation desire to come back in the next life with whiter skin as Aryans are at the top of the caste system.

Westerners are usually shocked to find this out. Westerners believe in the equality of the races because of their Christian background. Though many in the West are no longer practicing Christian, yet we have had the truth of God's Word taught for many centuries. The abolition movements of the 18th and 19th century were led by Bible-believing Christians like William Wilberforce and Abraham Lincoln. The world owes much of its present freedom to Christ and Christians. If we allow our Christian heritage to be stripped away from our Western schools and government and law, we will lose the very foundation of our culture, values and freedoms which Christians fought to lay for our blessed society. This is a danger for our children which we need to be aware of.

It is doubtful to me that the Gautama Buddha believed in reincarnation. Buddha was not a racist. Buddha did not believe in the Hindu caste system. Why else would a prince (highest caste) leave his palace to wander like a beggar (lowest caste)?

# Why do people believe Buddha taught reincarnation?

Reincarnation is a Hindu concept. Buddha rejected Hinduism. How then did reincarnation become such an integral part of Buddhism today? I can only suggest three possibilities.

Firstly, consider the possibility of misinterpretation. What Buddha clearly taught was the "cycle of suffering" – the cycle of life and death[6] – people suffer from birth to the grave. Christians would say people sin, people die. This is the obvious state of the present fallen world. Buddha reflected on the sufferings that came from old age, illness and death, and called this the "wheel of life". Could later Buddhists have misinterpreted this as the "wheel of reincarnation"? Easily. To say there is a cycle of life and death is not the same thing as saying monkeys are reborn as humans if they behave well or dark skin humans are reborn as white skin humans if they do good. Buddha was a man of reason and evidence, of which reincarnation has none.

Secondly, consider the historical factor. Since 200-1000 years lapsed between the time of Buddha and the actual writing of the *Tripitaka*, there was plenty of time for the dominant Hindu religion (the one Buddha was rejecting) to reassert its ideas back into Buddhism. Hinduism, being a pluralistic belief, is able to engulf other traditions it meets to preserve its own status in India.

Thirdly, consider the cultural factor. Buddha left Hinduism, but as a native of India he may have referred to Hindu ideas for the sake of his Hindu audience. Referring to reincarnation is not the same thing as approving of it! If reincarnation is thought through carefully, it does help people understand the heavy price of sin.

This cultural factor is congruent with Buddha's other teachings. For instance, Buddha would have known that eating meat or not eating meat will not take anyone to Heaven. He himself indulged after he came off his 6 year fast and started teaching "moderation". Yet he strongly advised his followers to avoid eating meat. What does vegetarianism have to do with the soul's salvation? Nothing. But it has everything to do with being sensitive to the Hindu culture in which Buddha lived.

Hinduism tells Indians that the cow is their god. If Buddhists living in India ate beef, they would be eating another person's god! You will find that Buddhists living outside of India do not struggle with the same cultural restriction. Nearly 100% of them eat meat, enjoy eating meat, and yet are perfectly happy to call themselves Buddhists. Vegetarianism was necessary for Buddhists living in a Hindu culture, but not elsewhere. I believe **Buddha would have treated reincarnation the same way he** treated vegetarianism, that is, put it in cultural perspective!

Until today we can see Buddha's wisdom in commanding to abstain from meat. Had Buddha disagreed openly with the Hindus, violence could have broken out - as it did in 1999, when Australian missionary Graham Staines was burnt alive with his 2 sons (aged 7 and 9) while they were sleeping in their station wagon in Orissa. Staines had been evangelizing and conducting aid work in India since 1965. The reason for the vicious murder? Convicted Dara Singh and Mahendra Hembram said it was the disrespect of Hinduism by converts who ate beef after becoming Christian!

The Apostle Paul offers this sound advice:

**1 CORINTHIANS 8:13**

**13 Therefore, if food makes my brother stumble** [because cultural factors make eating or drinking certain things offensive], **I will never again eat meat, lest I make my brother stumble.**

**ROMANS 14:19-21**

**19 Therefore let us PURSUE the things which make for PEACE** [including cultural sensitivity] **and the things by which one may edify** [build up] **another.**

**20 Do not destroy the work of God FOR THE SAKE OF FOOD. All things indeed are pure** [we can eat anything under the new covenant], **BUT it is evil for the man who eats with offense** [we should not eat anything without considering others' conscience].

**21 It is good NEITHER to EAT MEAT nor DRINK WINE nor do anything by which your brother stumbles or is offended or is made weak.**

**ROMANS 15:1-3**

**1 We then who are strong** [those who know freedom in Christ and know food doesn't affect our salvation are called 'strong'] **ought to bear with the scruples of the weak** [those who abide by many food restrictions are called 'weak'], **and not to please ourselves** [our freedom and strength are not to be abused, but used to help others].

**2 Let each of us please his neighbor** [including those from other cultures] **for his good, leading to edification.**

**3 For even Christ did not please Himself…**


Paul was certainly not a vegetarian, but like Buddha, he was a cultural pragmatist. If referring to the "unknown god" helped the Greek idol worshippers understand Christ, let's preach the "Unknown God"! If abstaining from beef or wine would help our Hindu or Muslim friend to accept Christ more easily, then why not abstain? Buddha would not have hesitated to use reincarnation as an illustration of the heavy price of sin, because his audience was Hindu. But how could he have subscribed to it when it is caste-based and racist?

# 17

# WOMEN IN BUDDHISM

In the previous chapter, we discussed how it shocks Westerners when they find out that the doctrine of reincarnation is racist. Yet another shock to Westerners is that the doctrine of reincarnation is also **sexist**.

It is always preferable to be reincarnated as a man than a woman. That's one reason why Chinese parents have been known to throw away their baby girls, long before the communists' "one birth policy"[1]. Women do not have the same status as men. Buddhist nuns have 311 laws to keep, while monks have 227. Since women are considered inferior, they have 84 more laws to control their flesh than men!

A menstruating woman cannot enter the temple or go near a monk; she is unclean. A woman can never give food directly into a monk's hands, nor can she receive anything directly from a monk. (A man can do both.) A woman has to pick things up from the floor, not from a monk. There is no gender equality in Buddhism.

Fully ordained nuns remain rare in Buddhism. When Sri Lanka recognized a fully ordained Buddhist nun in 1998, it made the news! Until today, Thailand does not recognize fully ordained nuns[2], but some feminists are going out to create their own *sangha* (religious community) anyway.

Christianity has long taught that every person is equal before God. *"There is neither Jew nor Greek, there is neither slave nor free, there is NEITHER MALE NOR FEMALE; for you are ALL ONE in CHRIST JESUS"* (Galatians 3:28). The Bible recognizes women in leadership and in ministry. Biblical values are literally thousands of years ahead of our time.

Some people don't believe this because they read in other passages where wives are told to obey their husbands. They misinterpret this as sexist. But the same passages also tell employees to obey their bosses! Peter and Paul were not telling husbands to lord it over their wives any more than they were telling bosses to lord it over their employees. We are all equal in value, yet we all play different roles at home and at work. This is orderly. This doesn't mean we are less valuable or less important. God loves us all the same. The way to salvation is exactly the same for a woman as for a man, for a Jew as for a Gentile. *"For there is no distinction between Jew and Greek, for the same Lord over all is rich to ALL who call upon Him"* (Romans 10:12).

## QUESTIONS & ANSWERS

# What is the Dalai Lama's public view on reincarnation?

This is an interesting question. In the early part of 2008, preceding the Olympic Games in China, Tibetan Buddhists staged a violent protest against the Chinese government. In an attempt to keep Buddhists on a path of non-violence, the Dalai Lama threatened to "resign" if the violence escalated.

Politically, this was a savvy move, showing the Chinese government that his aim is not independence, but Tibetans living "side by side" with the Chinese. Theologically, however, how could it be possible for him to resign as the 14<sup>th</sup> reincarnation of Guan Yin?

What's more puzzling is how the aged Dalai Lama, in his 70s, is preparing for his eventual death. The political question for millions of Tibetans and Chinese is, "What will happen after he dies?" The Dalai Lama has suggested that "there be a world referendum among the world's Tibetan Buddhists on whether he should be reincarnated. If the vote was in favour, he said that he might appoint a reincarnation while he was still alive, instead of being reborn as a boy after his death."[3]

While no one would argue that choosing a successor before he dies would be the most politically expedient solution, this begs at least two questions about his belief in reincarnation itself: 1) Who has the power to choose his own reincarnation *before* he dies? Even Buddha did not have that power; 2) How can other people vote on your reincarnation? Buddha never taught this, so where does it come from?

If the head of one of the major sects of Buddhism is ambivalent about reincarnation, I can tell you that most Buddhists I meet are too. Many Buddhists don't expect to be reincarnated, but believe their eternal soul will go to Heaven or Hell after death. This cannot be washed away from people's conscience by religious upbringing because God has "put eternity in their hearts" (Ecclesiastes 3:11). We all sense that after death, it is not over for us.

18

# KING ASOKA & THE PYTHON

## THREE STORIES FOR CROSS-CULTURAL COMMUNICATION

Let's look at three stories from Buddhism which explain how closely related the concepts of karma and sin truly are. You can use these stories any time to explain to Buddhists the similarities between Buddhism and Christianity. Of all the Buddhist stories, these should be emphasized the most, but rarely are by Westerners. Your eyes will be among the first to read it translated in your own language. Are you ready for this?

The first is the story of *King Asoka & the Python*

Next the story of the *Blind Turtle*

The third comes from the last words of Buddha, containing a series of stories of *The Brahman who asked to be free from karma, The Angel & the Stone* and *The Gongjak & Lightning Bug*.

You can use these three stories any time with a Buddhist or any person who believes in karma.

. . .

Buddha taught that there are 10 worst karmas or the 10 ways of death: namely, 3 physical karmas, 4 verbal karmas, and 3 mental karmas. (Notice the word karma is in each case understood in the negative sense of *bad* karma, and is nearly always so.) Just in case we think there is a little wiggle room out of Buddha's 10 commandments, the following story is an explicit example of a mental sin. This Buddhist story gives the penalty for having even one of the least of these karmas. It's a well known story you can use with any Buddhist.

### King Asoka & the Python

This is the story of King Asoka's father turning into a snake. Many Buddhist stories are told in parables, so you don't have to accept them as literal facts. Parables illustrate a truth that Buddhism teaches.

First of all, you may be wondering who King Asoka is. He was an ancient Indian king who came to the throne by killing all his half-brothers' and leaving only his one full brother alive. Asoka became a Buddhist convert. His name is known among Buddhists because he is credited with spreading Buddhism about 200 years after Buddha died. His name in Pali-Sanskrit is *Ashoka* or "without sorrow". His full title in Thai is *Praya-Asoke-Maha-Raj*, which may be transliterated as "Pharaoh Happy Great Raj." King Asoka is a very important figure in Buddhist history. This is a legend associated with him.

When King Asoka's father was still alive, he was a good man who kept all the commandments[1], prayed always and never failed to give alms to the poor. He searched for a way to escape sin and go to Nirvana. He sincerely adored the

ways of Buddha and strictly kept all Buddha's
commandments. Many times in his life he donated gifts to
the monks and to the temple.

One day he was cutting across a farm on his way to the
temple. He happened to see many little fish[2] in a puddle of
water. He thought to himself, "If I caught these fish, they
would make a nice dish of marinated fish.[3] He only thought
this in his heart but he did not obey his intention.

Not long after that he, being old, died a natural death.
When his spirit arrived at the gates of Heaven, the angel who
kept the gates of Heaven said, "You must pay for your sins
first or else you cannot enter Heaven." The father of King
Asoka became a python that dwelt in the Himmapan jungle,
eating fish and other living animals.

When King Asoka ascended to the throne instead of his
father, he was also a good man who faithfully kept all the
commandments. He succeeded in learning all the teachings[4]
of Buddha until he was able to fly and walk on air. After he
died and departed from this earth, he went up to Heaven. He
asked the angel who kept the gates of Heaven where his
father was, for he longed for him. The angel answered, "Your
father has gone to pay for his sin since he violated the
commandment and is now a big snake living in Himmapan
jungle eating fish and other living animals. If you want to see
your father, you must go back and find him in Himmapan
jungle."

When the python saw his son, he did not recognize him
and said to himself, "This is my food." (The story assumes
that King Asoka is no longer in human form, but in some
animal form.) Before he could eat him, his son called to him,
"I was your son when you used to be a human." The snake
challenged him, "If you were truly my son, then prove it by
walking on my back from head to tail. If you can do it
without falling off, then truly you are my son. But if you fall

off, I will eat you until nothing is left because you are my food."

The son moved up and down the snake's back many times without falling. Then the son asked the snake, "How is it that when you were human, you kept many commandments and were generous to the needy, yet did you not receive any merit[5] in return?"

The father told his son, "Your father violated the commandment to not kill.[6] I only thought to kill in my heart without committing the act, and for that mental sin I have to become a python to pay for my sin in Himmapan jungle."

Therefore the son asked the father, "How long will it take you to pay for your sin?"

The father replied, "If my son wants to know how long, then let him count how many scales are on my back. According to the number of scales on my back, that's how many times I must come back to suffer and pay for my sin!"

One lifetime per scale. It's obvious Buddha defined sin and warned of the horrible repercussions of sin.

He taught it in such a way that many people assume he taught reincarnation, but I don't think it can be proven that Buddha himself believed in reincarnation. He simply taught that one lifetime of doing good deeds and avoiding bad deeds is not enough to erase your sins. He said it would take you lifetimes. If you were as good King Asoka's father, which would be pretty tough to beat, you would still have to come back as many times as there are scales on a snakes back, and there are a lot of scales on a snakes back! I've never counted, but I'm sure there are hundreds. That's a lot of suffering.

The New Model Thai-English Dictionary Volume II (1984) actually defines this vicious cycle *wattasongsan* as "eternal suffering". Why would it be called *eternal* if we can keep coming back in an ever improved state until we are finally so good we escape? Buddha never taught us to trifle with karmic revenge by imagining its consequences are *temporary*. The truth is everyone born is imprisoned in sin, which leads to *eternal suffering*.

Buddha had such a deep revelation of personal sin that I suppose it would be difficult for anyone who doesn't understand sin to understand him. His insight is reminiscent of Martin Luther's in the 1500s. Everyone can comment on the evils of the world, but Luther was disturbed by his own wretched state. Publicly he was a monk of good standing in the *Roman* Catholic Church, but privately he was tormented by the thought of what might happen to him when he faced his God on the Day of Judgment. It drove Luther to the Bible where he found his answer in Paul's letter to the *Romans,* appropriately enough! (If you have a Bible, read the entire book of Romans for yourself! It will change your life.)

In 500BC, a contemporary of Buddha had a similar insight. It was Socrates who said to Plato, "It may be that Deity can forgive sins, but I do not see how!" How can a just God ignore justice and allow our sins to go unpunished? What can we offer to atone for our sins? And who can pay the just price? The best of minds have searched the answer, but never found it.

Their best conclusion seems to allude to reincarnation, only because they did not see how one sinner's life can pay for his ever increasing debt of sin. It may surprise many Christians to know that Jesus taught a similar parable as the Story of *King Asoka & the Python.* I will address this in detail in the next two chapters.

# 19

# JESUS ON REINCARNATION

I believe that reincarnation is one of the best teachings found anywhere outside the Bible. Yes, you read that correctly. Don't put this book in the fire, Christians! Let me explain. Reincarnation is one of the best doctrines Buddhism is known for. I think it is a great friend to us who are Christians.

Most followers of Eastern religion do not question, "Why should you be reincarnated? Why does Buddhism teach you have to be reincarnated?" They will not raise these questions in Western classes on Buddhism.

What is the point of the Buddhist teaching that we should be reincarnated, and usually in a *worse* state or *lower* form? The answer is simple. Because of our karma or our sins! In this context, these words mean exactly the same thing.

Our sin is so bad, our karma is so heavy, we cannot pay for it in one life-time. The fact that you are born, according to Buddha, is proof you're a sinner. If you weren't a sinner, if you were perfectly good in a previous life, you wouldn't be born at all. You would "go *nippan*" or reach nirvana, which means you would cease from existence, you would go extinct.

That is the Buddhist version of Heaven: that you no longer come back but are exempt from the vicious cycle of life.

A Sri Lankan who came to our church and received Christ told me: "My grandmother is a strong Buddhist. She taught me when I was little, 'You're born into sin. It's a sinful thing to be born because your mother suffered. As soon as you're born into life, you're born into sin. Even when you live, it's sin. When you die, it's sin. And then you start again.'"

As we saw illustrated in the Parable of King Asoka & the Python, Buddhism teaches that no amount of good work in this life alone can pay for our karma. You would have to be reborn again and again to pay for it. The problem with that is every time you are born you sin some more, so you're adding sins to your account. You're in constant deficit.

Think of it in financial terms: some people's financial decisions have put them into such debt than the interest is running higher than they could ever catch up to. The debt is growing faster than they can make money to repay, even with two jobs or overtime. So they live their life constantly trying to service their debt. Sin is like debt, Buddhism teaches. You can *tam boon*[1] all your life just to service your karma, but you will never quite win in this catch-up game. You are trapped inside a vicious cycle of sin and suffering.

## FINANCIAL DEBT & REINCARNATION

Jesus agrees with this assessment. He compares moral deficit to financial deficit. Before we go to Jesus' parable to see how Jesus might view reincarnation, we need to understand that the current problem of "deficit spending" by the governments and people in the First World is going to cost not only the present generation, but also the next generation. The present generation seems to be enjoying the irresponsible lifestyle of living on borrowed money, but this lack of financial control will catch up and bite the next generation in the heels. The national debts of America and Japan now stand at roughly US$8 trillion each! Believe it or not, this enormous government debt is seen as the indirect debt of every tax payer! The good intentions and hard work of one generation will simply not be enough to solve this deficit spending, it is going to cause future generations to suffer. In this sense, any good fiscal conservative is a believer in economic reincarnation. Though the original spender dies, his debt must live on and get passed on to the next generation in some other shape or form. Debt goes to economic Nirvana when it ceases to exist or is extinguished.

The practical question for everyone is: Since a spender will not stop spending, even after he's bankrupt, can a bankrupt person spend his way out of bankruptcy? Likewise, the best minds in the world have asked: **Since a sinner will not stop sinning, can his "sinning less" make his sin problem go away?** Can a sinner sin his way out of sin?

We can all see where this is going. The only way some people will ever get out of debt is if their creditor forgives their debt, at a great cost to themselves. But someone is going to have to suffer!

Buddha correctly identified the problem of humanity. It is the heavy price of our sin. Jesus completely agrees. However, Buddha never offered a solution. He may have hinted at it, as we shall see in the last words of Buddha. Buddha only left with these parting words, "Don't pray to me. Don't worship idols."

So God sent Jesus Christ 500 years after Buddha because He loves Buddhists. Many wise teachers came before Jesus, but Jesus came with wisdom and power from Heaven. Buddha taught for 45 years, Socrates for 40, Plato for 50, Aristotle for 40, but Jesus for only 3. Yet the worldwide impact of Jesus' 3-year ministry far outweighs the combined 175 years of teaching by these men who were among the greatest thinkers the world has ever seen.

Christians do not realize that Jesus taught a parable that is very similar to the Buddhist Parable of *King Asoka and the Python*, but in more precise terms. Jesus amplifies what Buddhism suggested. Jesus actually tells us the *exact* amount of spiritual debt a sinner owes to God... and *exactly* how many lives you would owe, if you were to pay it yourself. Let's take a look at what Jesus, the greatest teacher in the world, has to say in the Gospel of Matthew.

# THE KING & THE UNGRATEFUL DEBTOR

Jesus taught one parable that can be misconstrued as teaching on "reincarnation". Buddhists love to hear this story. It's a parable found in Matthew 18 about how many days and lives a sinner owes to God!

**MATTHEW 18:23-35**

**23 Therefore the kingdom of Heaven is like a certain king...**

It is worthy to mention that the sages liked kings! Both Buddha and Jesus liked to bring up kings because most people in the world understand kings and kingdoms.

**23 Therefore the kingdom of Heaven is like a certain king who wanted to settle accounts with his servants.**

**24 And when he had begun to settle accounts, one was brought to him who owed him TEN THOUSAND TALENTS.**

**25 But as he was NOT ABLE TO PAY, his master commanded that he be sold, with his wife and children and all that he had, and that payment be made.**

When a person is in debt and cannot pay, he has to sell everything that belongs to him and keep working until the debt is settled. This particular servant's debt was so deep that he could not afford to repay it even with his life. The king required his life to be sold, and the lives of his wife and his children, too. It sounds a lot like what Buddhism is saying: one life is not enough!

**26 The servant therefore FELL DOWN** [this is what we are supposed to do] **before him, saying, 'Master, have patience with me, and I will pay you all.'**

**27 Then the master of that servant was moved with compassion, RELEASED him, and FORGAVE him the debt.**

**28 But that servant went out and found one of his fellow servants who owed him a HUNDRED DENARAII** [much less than ten thousand talents]; **and he laid hands on him and took him by the throat, saying, 'Pay me what you owe!'** [He threatened him.]

**29 So his fellow servant FELL DOWN at his feet and begged him, saying, 'Have patience with me, and I will pay you all.'**

**30 And he would not, but went and threw him into PRISON till he should pay the debt.**

Now understand that when you owe a debt, it is within the rights of the creditor to have you put in prison. The creditor really didn't do anything wrong, because if you have a debt that you haven't paid on time, you belong in prison. And the Bible would agree that if you have sin, you belong in spiritual prison. But now watch the twist of the story.

**31 So when his fellow servants saw what had been done, they were very grieved, and came and told their master all that had been done.**

**32 Then his master, after he had called him, said to him, 'You wicked servant! I forgave you ALL THAT DEBT** [we're going to figure how big this debt was] **because you begged me.**

**33 Should you not also have had compassion on your fellow servant, just as I had pity on you?'**

**34 And his master was angry, and delivered him to the torturers** [that's what we experience when we ignore debt – torture!] **until he should pay all that was due to him.**

**35 So My Heavenly Father also will do to you if each of you, from his heart, does not forgive his brother his trespasses."**

Whenever you read the Bible, the best thing you can do is to put yourself in the story. The mistake we tend to make when we read the Bible and don't understand it is to assume, "This applies to someone else." No, this story is about us!

Who's the king? God Himself is the King in this story. Who is the servant that owes ten thousand talents? That's us. By parable, Jesus is comparing our accountability to the world's financial system to our responsibility to God's spiritual system. "The kingdom of God is like this." The Bible says that we owe God ten thousand talents of debt for each of our sins. Now let's find out how much that is.

1 talent = 60 minas.

1 mina = 100 denarii.

Now if you cross reference the Bible, you'll find out that in another parable, in Matthew chapter 20, the master agreed with the laborers to pay each of them a denarius per day for their labor. So a denarius is equivalent to "one day's wage."

Now let's do the math: 1 talent equals 60 minas. 1 minas equals 100 denarii. 1 denarius equals a day's wage. That means 1 talent equals 6,000 denarii (60 minas x 100 denarii) or 6,000 days' worth of wages. Therefore 10,000 talents equal 60 million denarii or days of labor.

Other Scriptures corroborate this calculation. In the Old Testament, King Amaziah of Judah hired 100,000 soldiers from the northern kingdom of Israel. How much did he pay for so many soldiers?

**2 CHRONICLES 25:6**

**6 He also hired one hundred thousand mighty men of**

valor from Israel for ONE HUNDRED TALENTS of silver.

One hundred thousand soldiers agreed to go to war for one hundred talents. Let's see if that was fair wage: 1 talent equals 6000 denarii, so 100 talents equal 600,000 denarii. Divide that by the number of soldiers and each soldier was paid 6 denarii or 6 days' worth of wages. Since Amaziah pre-paid these men before they ever went to battle, 6 days' wages seem a very fair deposit. None of them ended up fighting because a prophet averted war, so Amaziah lost his deposit and 100,000 men kept 100 talents!

Each sinner owes not 100 talents, but 10,000 talents or 60 million denarii! This is what Jesus taught. Let's pause for a second, as this is extremely important. How long is a life? If you live 100 years, how long is your life in term of days?

A year has 365 days. That means that if you're alive for 100 years, you have 36,500 days. The Bible reminds us that life is short. "For what is your life? It is even a vapor that appears for a little time and then vanishes away" (James 4:14).

How short is your life in term of days? For most readers, you probably have less than 15,000 days left. And you have no guarantee of tomorrow.

Life is extremely short.

Let's say we give you a lot of grace, and suppose that you are capable of working from the day that you're born till the day that you die. You take no rest. You work seven days a week. How many lifetimes will it take for you to pay this debt of 60 million denarii?

Let me make the calculation for you. The days of work owing, divided by the days of a single life, equals the number of lifetimes required to pay the current debt of sin, assuming no more debt is incurred in future lifetimes. Are you ready?

It will take you 1,643.8 lives. Since you cannot be born 80%, we'll round up the total. It will take you 1,644 lives of continuous work, seven days a week, from the day you're born until the day you die, to pay off your sins. That's how much you owe.

Now that is only how much one person owes. Currently, we have 6 billion people. So 1,644 lifetimes worth of perfect work multiplied by six billion human beings ...the total human debt is now worth 9,864 billion lives worth of perfect work 7 days a week.[1]

Let's translate that into days instead of lifetimes. Each person owes 60 million days of perfection, multiplied by six billion human beings, equals 3.6 billion, billion days or $36 \times 10^{16}$ days. Since Creation, there have only been 2.2 *million* days. Humanity would need 3.6 *billion, billion* days to pay off its runaway debt to God.

What is Jesus saying to us? Exactly what Buddha was teaching. It is impossible for you to rid yourself of sin by your own good works. All you can do is fall at the Master's feet and say, "Lord, have mercy on me, because I have not enough to pay and I am going straight to Hell. I cannot boast that I go to church. I cannot boast that I've been water baptized. I cannot boast that I've read this book or studied many religions."

On the Day of Judgment, I won't be able to help you. I'm glad you're reading my book, but I can't help you. I owe the same debt you do. All I've done is fallen at the Master's feet like this servant in the parable and said, "Jesus, please have mercy on me. I have wronged you and I've wronged others, and the debt is accumulating every day. I cannot pay, but I know You can."

Whereas Buddha offered no solution, God sent Jesus Christ to die 2,000 years ago. The most amazing fact about the Gospel is that in *3 days*, Jesus paid the entire debt of humanity in full! This begs the question: "How come? How come Jesus could pay *everybody*'s debt, which amounts to billions and billions of days' worth of perfect work, and do it in only 3 days? How did He manage to pay off so much?"

In fact, I want to let you know, Jesus overpaid for you. He paid too much!!

What we try to do is not enough. But what Jesus did is too much!! Why is that? Think with me. For those of you who run your own business, you're going to get this straightaway. For those of you who are employed, you'll get it too.

The standard work day is 8 hours a day. The Hebrews actually divided the ideal day into 3 parts: 8 hours of sleep[2], 8 hours of work, 8 hours of family time and leisure. So most people have 8 hours a day to work. I understand some people work longer hours, but nobody can work 16 hours a day for the rest of their lives. So in any city or country, any farm or firm, everybody has about 8 hours a day to work.

Q uestion: Why is it that the CEO of a company can earn so much more income than a salesman? They both have 8 hours a day to work. They both have the same physical limitations. They clock in at the same time. They clock out at the same time. How come the CEO makes $200,000 a year while the salesman works just as hard and only makes $40,000 a year?

Why? Different positions. The CEO has a higher rank. He doesn't have more time. And not all CEOs have more talent either. But because of the position, his time is worth a lot more.

Australia and New Zealand were the first countries in the world to enact minimum wage laws in 1896. As of 2007, the minimum wage in Australia is AU$13.47 per hour, or US$11.57 per hour. That is how much a minimum wage earner's time is valued. Compare that to former President Bill Clinton's hourly fees. In 2006, President Clinton made

US$10.2 million for giving 57 speeches.[3] That translated to nearly US$180,000 per speech. If Bill Clinton spoke for 45 minutes during each speech, that would mean he was paid US$4000 for each minute he spoke! Why is he paid so much? Does he have more time than the minimum wage earner? No. He has a higher position.

For those who come from kingdoms, you will understand this. In Thailand, the Princess of Thailand - not the queen, just the princess – is often invited to various Grand Opening ceremonies. There, photographers and a yellow ribbon await her. When she cuts the yellow ribbon, do you know how much she is paid? 2 million baht. That's around AU$75,000 or US$64,000. She graces the ceremony, she cuts a ribbon, two million baht is due her, she goes home. Why is her time worth so much? She has the second highest position in the land. She is the daughter of the King.

You and I, on other hand, may work 8 hours a day, every day for an entire year, yet still not get 2 million baht. Why? Lower status. The Princess has a higher status, so that's why her time is worth more.

If you understand this, you will understand why I encourage every Christian to search the Scriptures that tell you who you are in Christ and confess them every day. If you understand the position that you have in Christ, you will understand why many wise Christians can work with no sweat, no stress, and no worry, yet become richer than sinners and more blessed than their colleagues. We may put in the same hours, but I have a higher position. I'm the son of the CEO of Heaven. So if I believe I have been made an heir of God and joint heir of Christ[4], I am more than a conqueror through Christ[5], and I am seated in Heavenly places in Christ Jesus[6], then God should be able to bless me more, not only financially, but in my health, my family, and my relationships.[7] No parent ever loved their child more than God the Father loves us.

With the above understanding of position, time, and value, let's return to Jesus' call and accomplishment. God the Father looked down on earth and saw the debt of the world. He searched but found nobody who could pay for it. No one was worthy. In fact, there's not enough gold buried in the entire world to exchange for the debt of sin owing to God.

And so God said, "I'm going to have to send the Lord of Heaven Himself." Hebrews 7:26 says that Jesus is "higher than the Heavens." You understand, of course, that the Owner of Heaven is worth more than Heaven itself. So Heaven and earth did not have enough to pay. But the Lord of Heaven came down to earth and said, "With My time, with My life, I will pay for all of your sins."

Jesus came to pay for six billion people's sins, plus those of all the others who were born before us. Jesus said, "I'll do it in three days. In fact, I'll over pay."

The first day the Lord of the Universe spent in Hell was enough. As the Highest Authority above all royalties and governments, even a second of his time is worth more than all the powers of this world. One day should have been enough. Three days in Hell was over-redemption! It is our guarantee that nothing is left owing. He has fully redeemed us from Satan and we are now His. All sins – past, present and future – are completely expunged. In Christ, not only is the believer forgiven, but blessed overwhelmingly, and preserved securely for His glorious Coming. That's what Jesus accomplished which no-one else could do.

## QUESTION & ANSWER

**I**s there a God in Buddhism?
Buddha never denied the existence of God. His teachings are deeply rooted in the assumption that there is

absolute morality and there is a just distribution of merits and demerits. This strongly implies the presence of an Intelligent, Personal and Moral God. Otherwise, who is keeping track of every person's moral decisions and the distribution of rewards and punishment?

**Morality without Personality is an impossibility.** It would take not only a moral Person to keep count of everybody's thoughts, words and actions, but also a very intelligent Person to keep track of karma. This Being would have to be All-Seeing, All-Knowing, and Perfectly Just. Is this not, by definition, belief in a Moral Omniscient God?

In Thai Buddhism, there is a title used to refer to God: *Sing Saksit Nai Sakolaloak*. Thai Buddhists know this refers to "Something Holy in the Universe." When Buddhists pray, they will often pray to *Sing Saksit Nai Sakolaloak*. So they do actually pray to the Supreme Being, only they don't know His Name is Jesus Christ.

This is similar to the idolatrous Athenians praying to the *Unknown God*. The Athenian religion was certainly not centered around the *Unknown God*, but neither could it deny His existence. Paul highlighted what they considered minor and declared, "The One whom you worship without knowing, Him I proclaim to you" (Acts 17:23).

The Bible says that every child is born with the knowledge of God – they are "alive unto God" (Romans 7:9). No child is born with an "I don't believe in God" gene. No child dies and goes to Hell. They all go to Heaven. Only after social conditioning, peer pressure and religious indoctrination does a child accept human theories and deny God. But even then, for the rest of his life, a person lives with an awareness of Eternity (Ecclesiastes 3:11) and of the coming Judgment (Romans 2:15-16).

## THE BLIND TURTLE

I promised to give you three Buddhist stories you can share with any Buddhist. You've got the first story – the Story of King Asoka & the Python. You can use that to explain the cost of karma, even *one* mental karma! Do you remember that now?

Let me give you the second story, a nice little short one, which you can use in cross-cultural communication between Buddhists and Christians. In this one, Buddha described the way to escape. It is about the Blind Turtle.

One day Buddha's disciples came and asked him. "What rules should we follow to escape from our sins?"

Buddha replied, "How shall you be set free from your sins? Put a yoke in the river and let it float down a stream for three years, and after three years, release a blind turtle to go after that yoke. The day the blind turtle finds the yoke is the day when your sins will be forgiven."

What was Buddha saying? His point was it's impossible to save yourself from your own sins by trying to keep good rules. The likelihood of your going to Heaven by trying to be good is the same as that of a blind turtle finding a yoke after it's been dropped in a flowing river and disappeared for three years. Can you see Buddha understood the heavy price of sin? He saw some things that are quite Biblical. The Bible teaches us, "Do not try to save yourself. You need the Savior to save you. You are not the Savior! You are a sinner. Repent and believe Jesus Christ."

The third story contains a prophecy that will be the most startling of them all.

QUESTION & ANSWER

W as Buddha sinless?
Buddha abandoned his young wife and new born child. If I abandoned my wife and child, would it not be considered a very bad sin? *"There is none who does good, no, not one"* (Psalm 14:3).

No one is sinless except Jesus. *"You know that He was manifested to take away our sins, and in Him there is no sin"* (1 John 3:5).

# THE LAST WORDS OF BUDDHA

Before Buddha left this earth, he left his last commandments to his disciples. I will transliterate the Pali first, then translate the meaning into English:

*Appa-mano*! Do not make idols nor worship and bow down to them.

*Jata-rako*! Seek the Holy One who is always living.

*Appama-pana-sumba-taypa*! Watch your heart. Don't be careless, but be ready all the time.

*Vi-mut-ti*! Let all of you search for the way to escape your sinful nature[1], or else eternal ruin will come to all of you.

Buddha continued to command his disciples, saying, "To worship correctly, you should worship the truth, don't worship materially (Pali: *a-mi-ta-bucha*). This has no value."

Many Buddhists are tired of buying material things to worship their material idols. They have to buy incense and candles and gold foils and food. One elderly Buddhist who became Christian said, "God wants us to worship him right here in our hearts. That's what He wants more than anything – our hearts!"

One of the most interesting last words of Buddha was to

"seek the Holy One who is always living". Does Buddhism have more to say about this Person?

## THE OLD BRAHMAN AND BUDDHA

It is common knowledge among Buddhists that Buddha prophesied the coming of a Savior after him. He is called the *Maitreya* in Sanskrit, *Metteya* in Pali and *Pra-med-trai*[2] in Thai. He is expected to be a world teacher and a world ruler who will end death!

If we can achieve liberation by keeping Buddha's laws, making merit, or meditating, what need would there be for a *Maitreya*? But a *Maitreya* makes perfect theological sense if Buddha did not see himself as the solution for mankind's sins. It makes sense that Buddha told his followers not to look to him, but to look for another Holy One, just as John the Baptist did. Buddha was a very humble person.

Buddha's prophecies of the *Maitreya* are scattered in many places. Some were passed down orally. Some were recorded on palm leaves. Buddha's prophecy may have once been in the Thai Tripitaka, but some have told me that this passage has been ripped out of the sacred texts, because it is all too clear who it is referring to. I cannot confirm or deny this rumour. All I can say is the following version was found by former monk *Tongsuk Siriruk* in *Kampee Khom*, meaning the Cambodian or Khmer Canon, so we have the Cambodians to thank for preserving this text for us. Thai Buddhism came from the Khmer people, so it is reasonable to expect that the earliest, unabridged stories of Buddha would be found in the Khmer Canon. Listen and see if it sounds familiar.

When Buddha was traveling in this life, an old Brahman priest[3] dressed in white came to ask Buddha, "How can a human or a priest follow all the commandments and escape from all his sins?"

Buddha replied, "Even if you gave alms to the poor, donated gifts to the monks, kept all the commandments up to *seen* five, *seen* eight, *seen* ten, *seen* 227, even up to 99 million, even if you lifted your hands to the sky in worship and offered yourself as a burnt offering, and prayed 5 times a day, **still you cannot save yourself from your sins.** If you did this every day your good deeds would be worth no more than a strand of baby hair still in its mother's womb for 8 months[4]. It is not even good enough to get close to the gates of Heaven.

Our good deeds, no matter how much we do, is worth so little! Doesn't this sound like the "Love Chapter" of the Bible? In 1 Corinthians 13, the Holy Spirit tells us that "though I bestow all my goods to feed the poor, and though I give my body to be burned, but have not love, it profits me nothing."

The Bible teaches that the standard to go to Heaven is to love always. That means to love God with all our heart, soul, mind and strength, and to always put him first in every decision. There is not one human being alive who has always done that!

Next it means to love our neighbor as ourselves. We don't have to look too far, just start with our own father and mother, start with our own husband or wife, then go on to our other neighbors. There is no human being alive, be they Catholic, Christian, Protestant, Buddhist, Hindu or Muslim, who has ever loved God and their neighbor all the time, even as themselves.

Even if we give to the poor, raise our hands to the sky in worship, offer our bodies to be burned as an offering, but fail to love, all of our sacrifice amounts to nothing because we will lose our soul in Hell. We have got to pay for the sins we commit. Sins cannot be washed away, except by Jesus' blood.

That's why many have turned to Him and put their trust in Him. But let's continue with the old Brahman. He was obviously startled by Buddha's answer, so he pressed in further.

The old Brahman continued to ask, "If this is so, what must we do to escape and be safe from sins?"

## THE STORY OF THE ANGEL & THE STONE

Buddha replied, "The sins of humanity are many and heavy, it's heavier than the sky and thicker than the earth. It's thicker than a large granite stone used for burial, one foot thick on every side. Imagine if an angel came down from Heaven and gave this stone a sweep with his cloth once a year, the day that this stone completely disappears is the day man's sins and karma will disappear."

Do you see Buddha's point? Suppose you've got a large granite stone, and you give it one sweep per year with a frail cloth, the day that the stone disappears is the day your sins will disappear!

Buddha continued, "I myself have left all my princely inheritance, abandoned lust and became a monk. I esteem that my good deeds are not few. I hold onto the 8 commandments, even up to 100,000. If I could do this and give away everything I have for 10 lives, yet I still cannot get over one of my sins."

Buddha understood the problem of sin. He found the problem in his spirit, and simply tried to explain it in his own words to the people living at that time. I believe that he was preparing the way for Jesus to come because he lived about 500 years before Christ.

It's important to note here that Buddhists commonly claim that Siddhartha Gautama is the 10th reincarnation of the same person. But Buddha did not say that he was the 10th reincarnation, he only said that even if he could live sacrificially for 10 lives, he still could not erase his sins.

We have a similar mistake sometimes taught in Christianity. In their young days, Peter and John had a bit of a rivalry, so Peter asked Jesus about John's calling. Jesus said to Peter, "If I will that he remain till I come, what is that to you? You follow Me." Then this saying went out among the brethren that this disciple would not die. Yet Jesus did not say to him that he would not die, but, "If I will that he remain till I come, what is that to you?" (John 21:21-23). The emphasis was not on John living eternally, the emphasis was on Jesus having the power of life! If Jesus would, He could call John to be a witness for 2000 years. It's Jesus' choice whom He wants to call for which assignment. So stop comparing yourself to your brother, stop comparing your job to another person's job, just follow Jesus!

Let's keep going.

The Brahman pressed on, "If this be the case, what must I do to get over all my sins?"

Buddha told him, "Let all of you do a good deed and seek for **another Holy One** who will come and save the world. He will rescue you in the near future."

The old Brahman asked, "This Holy One who will come and rescue the world in the near future, what does he look like?"

At this point of the story, I can't help but smile. I can imagine Asians asking this type of question in the middle of a sermon! "You say there's a Savior coming… Say, what does he look like? Long hair or short hair? Fat or skinny? Short or tall?" This story bears the marks of an authentic conversation that took place in ancient Asia!

## THE GONGJAK

Buddha replied, "The Holy One who will rescue the world in the near future will have scars in his hands and scars in his feet like the shape of a *gongjak*.[5] In His side, there is a stab wound. His forehead is full of blemish and scars. The Holy Person will be like a golden vessel, a very large one, that will carry you across the cycle of suffering until you pass over to Heaven Nippan[6].

Buddha did not use the word "Heaven" alone, but the combination of words "Heaven Nippan." The meaning of Buddha is very clear: once you reach this Heaven, you will not come back. Once in Heaven, you will certainly not be reincarnated. Many have failed to understand Buddha's teaching on the "cycle of suffering" and the "impossibility of paying for sins in one lifetime" as an observation of life and the seriousness of sin. They have interpreted this to mean Buddha taught the Hindu concept of reincarnation.

Buddha told the old Brahman, "The Holy Person will be like a golden vessel, a very large one, that will carry you across the cycle of suffering until you pass over to Heaven Nippan." In other words, cross over with Him and you will never come back to suffer. Listen carefully to Buddha's last words!

## THE LIGHTNING BUG

Do not pursue the old way, you will certainly not escape. Turn from your old ways, and you will have **a new spirit that shines like a lightning bug** come down from Heaven above and dwelling in your hearts. And you will be given victory over all your enemies, whether they come against you from four directions or eight directions. Nobody will by any means harm you and when you die, you will not come back to this world again.

Oh, my! Is it time for this message to go into all the world? I think it's possible Buddha was allowed in his last days to see Jesus. In a similar way to the disciples' encounter of Jesus in Acts 1:3, "He also presented Himself alive after His suffering by many infallible proofs, being seen by them during forty days and speaking of the things pertaining to the kingdom of God." No one can be dogmatic about what Buddha saw and didn't see. All I am saying is the likelihood of a man being able to describe the Savior with this precision without revelation from God is nigh zero.

In the Old Testament, many people saw Jesus Christ appear before His incarnation. If you didn't know that, you can do a study of it for yourself. On the one hand, no one can see God and live. Both the Old and New Testament confirms this: "Thou canst not see my face: for there shall no man see me, and live" (Exodus 33:20) and "No one has seen God at any time" (John 1:18). On the other hand, many people claimed to have seen Someone who shared all the attributes of God, variously called "God," "Lord," "the Angel of God," and "the Son of God." How can both positions be true? Because there are at least two Persons in the Godhead: God the Father, whom no man has seen, and God the Son, whom certain believers have been allowed to see throughout history.

Abraham met the LORD Jesus face to face (Genesis 18).

Jacob met Jesus face to face and recognized Him as Deity, "I have seen God face to face, and my life is preserved" (Genesis 32:30).

Ishmael's mother Hagar saw Jesus face to face, and called him both the "Angel of the Lord" and "Jehovah-Rohi," a Divine title meaning "God who sees" (Genesis 16:7-13).

Gideon saw Jesus as the "Angel of the Lord" but did not immediately recognized Him as Deity until he exclaimed for fear of his life, "Alas, O Lord God! For I have seen the Angel of the Lord face to face." The Lord assured him, "Peace be with you; do not fear, you shall not die" (Judges 6:11-23).

Samson's father Manoah met Jesus Christ and tried to ask for His Name. Interestingly Jesus withheld it. I believe it was because Mary was supposed to be the first person on earth to hear His Name. But Jesus did allude to one of His Divine titles "Wonderful," which is commonly understood as the title of the Messiah (Isaiah 9:6-7). Finally Manoah realized who was standing in front of him and told his wife, "We shall surely die, because we have seen God!" (Judges 13:21-23).

Even a heathen king, Nebuchadnezzar, saw Jesus Christ around the same time as Buddha. Nebuchadnezzar viciously threw three Hebrew children into a burning furnace but soon realized his mistake when God came to their rescue. Nebuchadnezzar rushed to his counselors and asked them, "Who is the fourth man in the burning oven, whose form is like the Son of God?" (Daniel 3:24-25). Nebuchadnezzar had seen Jesus Christ before He was incarnated! Jesus is not only human. He is God come in the flesh. He always existed. He is the Eternal One, the Creator, and He takes very special interest in humanity – visiting us, revealing Himself to us, and even dying for us.

There is a great likelihood, though I cannot prove it, that a man who was searching for truth named Siddhartha Gautama, while he was searching for a way to escape sin, saw Jesus either in a vision or a dream. Buddha tried to describe it the best way he could. "I saw scars in his hands and feet, like the holes of a *gongjak*, this ancient weapon that would tear your flesh apart." A *gongjak* is a very nasty spinning wheel with jagged edges. Buddha said, "I see the shape of this *gongjak* in His hands and in His feet."

Don't accept my opinion. Compare Buddha's words with John chapter 20 and see for yourself. Who was Buddha referring to?

JOHN 20:19-20, 22, 24-29 [After Jesus had risen from
the dead]

19 Then, the same day at evening, being the first day
of the week, when the doors were shut where the
disciples were assembled, for fear of the Jews, Jesus
came and stood in the midst, and said to them, "Peace be
with you."

20 Now when He had said this, He showed them HIS
HANDS and HIS SIDE. Then the disciples were glad
when they saw the Lord.

22 And when He had said this, He breathed on them,
and said to them, "RECEIVE the HOLY SPIRIT.

24 Now Thomas, called the Twin, one of the twelve,
was not with them when Jesus came.

25 The other disciples therefore said to him, "WE
HAVE SEEN THE LORD." So he said to them, "Unless I
see IN HIS HANDS the PRINT OF THE NAILS, and put
my finger into the PRINT OF THE NAILS, and put my
hand into HIS SIDE, I will not believe."

26 And after eight days His disciples were again
inside, and Thomas with them. Jesus came, the doors
being shut, and stood in the midst, and said, "Peace to
you!"

27 Then He said to Thomas, "Reach your finger here,
and LOOK AT MY HANDS; and reach your hand here,
and PUT IT INTO MY SIDE. Do not be unbelieving, but
believing."

28 And Thomas answered and said to Him, "My Lord
and my God!" [Jesus is not just a great prophet or teacher.
He is our Lord and God!]

29 Jesus said to him, "Thomas, because you have
seen Me, you have believed. [When Thomas recognized
Jesus as God, Jesus did not rebuke him. Jesus said, You have
believed correctly!] **Blessed are those who have not seen
and yet have believed."** [There are many people who have

not seen Jesus face to face, but believe in Him. They did not have to put their fingers through the nail print of His hands to put their trust in Him. Jesus said you are more blessed when you believe without seeing.]

I s it possible that Buddha in his search for true freedom saw a vision of Jesus Christ and at that moment put his trust in the Savior? He warned his disciples, "Do not pray to me. Do not follow your old ways [which was Hinduism and its associated idolatry]. If you do, you will not escape." Follow the new way and what will happen? You will be given a new spirit that shines like a lightning bug. Buddha's vision matches what Jesus gave the disciples in John 20:22, a new Spirit! The words are so amazingly similar to those of the prophets Ezekiel and Jeremiah, I invite you to compare them for yourself.

**EZEKIEL 36:25-27**

**25 Then I will sprinkle clean water on you, and you shall be clean; I will CLEANSE YOU from all your filthiness and FROM ALL YOUR IDOLS.**

**26 I will give you A NEW HEART and put A NEW SPIRIT within you; I will take the heart of stone out of your flesh and give you a heart of flesh.**

**27 I will put MY SPIRIT within you and cause you to walk in My statutes, and you will keep My judgments and do them.**

Both Ezekiel and Jeremiah prophesied of a new way (the new covenant) which will supersede the old and be ushered in by the Messiah. The distinguishing characteristic of the new way is this: whereas the old way tried to control human behavior through external laws (religion), the new way will guide human behavior by a changed heart or born again spirit (new birth)! Who can deliver this promise? Every person has a sinful spirit. Jesus alone has the Holy Spirit. So only Jesus can give us the Spirit that shines the Light of Life inside of our very core.

**JEREMIAH 31:31-33** [around 587 B.C.]

**31 Behold, the days are coming, says the LORD, when I will make a NEW COVENANT with the house of Israel and with the house of Judah--**

**32 not according to the** [old] **covenant that I made with their fathers in the day that I took them by the hand to lead them out of the land of Egypt** [the Exodus], **My covenant which they broke** [at Mount Sinai, they instantly broke the Ten Commandments by worshipping a golden calf], **though I was a husband to them, says the LORD.**

**33 But this is the** [new] **covenant that I will make with the house of Israel AFTER THOSE DAYS, says the LORD: I will put My law IN THEIR MINDS, and write it ON THEIR HEARTS; and I will be their God, and they shall be My people.**

Both Jeremiah and Ezekiel prophesied the same thing. One day, when we believe in the Messiah, God will reach down and take out our old heart of stone and He will give us a new heart. He will write His laws into the our mind and into our heart. He will give us a new spirit! Doesn't that sound like Buddha who said the Holy One will put a new spirit that shines like a lightning bug inside those who look for Him? The amazing thing is Ezekiel, Jeremiah and Buddha all lived around the same time!

I've found this to be true, when God gives me a message to share in church, many other pastors are getting the same message. Sometimes God gives us a unique message, but most of the time God has a message He wants to get out into the world at a particular time. How can many ministers around Australia and around the world, who often don't know each other, be receiving the same thing at the same time? Because it is the same Spirit of God who dwells in us. That's how I know there is a Holy Spirit. I know for sure that He lives in me and He lives in other believers. Though I cannot see the big picture the way He does, I can see that He coordinates His Church, especially the believers who are praying and listening. He has a message for the earth and for the churches and He calls on *you* to help get it out!

When I look back at history and think of Jeremiah, Ezekiel and Buddha, it doesn't surprise me that they all lived around 500BC and they all got a similar word, which was basically: "God says don't follow the old ways, follow the coming Savior and I will put a new spirit in you!" God had a message to send to all people around that time. I don't know how many more people in the world picked up that message in their spirits, but only two of them got to write it in the Word of God!

Is it sacrilege to think that Buddha may have compared the Holy Spirit to a lightning bug? Not if the Bible compares the Holy Spirit to a dove. "A spirit like a lightning bug," to Buddha, would have been the only way he could describe a Spirit that gives Light. The Bible says God "has delivered us from the power of DARKNESS, and translated us into the kingdom of his dear Son" (Colossians 1:13). In other words, Light will come into your life when you become Christian.

Buddha saw an event in the future, and said it looked to him like lightning bugs were all around those who believed. If Buddha was referring to the Holy Spirit, doesn't that demean the Holy Spirit? Doesn't that make Him small? One should go to the Book of Acts chapter 2, where the Holy Spirit was given in fulfillment of the words of the prophets, and re-read what the Bible says. The Bible records that 120 people were waiting for the Holy Spirit to come down, and 50 days after the Resurrection, do you know what happened? Just before they all got filled with the Holy Spirit, there appeared little tongues of fire on top of each of them! The

King James Version says "cloven tongues like as of fire." That means each was a divided tongue, not even a full tongue, but just a little tongue! According to the Book of Acts, that little tongue of light and of fire represented the Holy Spirit descending.

Could God not have shown Buddha a glimpse of the Day of Pentecost in advance and Buddha, not being completely inspired, reported, "It looks like little lightning bugs!" I am not claiming Buddha was inspired in the same way as the writers of the Bible, but listen to the essence of what he was communicating! His charge to his followers were, "Do not follow the old ways. Wait for what is coming! Wait for the best! You will not only get your sins washed, you will get a new spirit that gives light inside of you." To that, we can all say, Amen!

The wisest men on earth have given us these promises. Don't follow the old ways. I tell Buddhists, "Open up your heart today. All you need to do is repent and believe in Jesus. If you want to know if God is real, if you want to know if Jesus can forgive you of your sins and give you a brand new spirit, pray this prayer that will change your life and bring a new spirit into you. You will never be the same again and you will know that God is real and Jesus loves you."

## A PRAYER FOR GOD'S GIFT OF SALVATION

The most exciting part of sharing Jesus with Buddhists is praying with them to receive salvation. If you don't know how to pray that, you might like to use the one below. I believe that whenever someone prays this prayer sincerely, all their sins will be washed away and the power of the Holy Spirit will come:

*"Dear Heavenly Father, I'm sorry for my sins. I believe Jesus died on the Cross to pay for the penalty of my karma and the punishment of my sins. I believe that on the third day, Jesus rose again from the dead, victorious over Satan, the enemy of my soul. I now accept Jesus as my Lord and Savior. Thank You for forgiving me and accepting me as Your child, I pray in Jesus' Name."*

The moment someone sincerely puts his trust in Christ to save him, his sins are wiped away and he is born again. It's important to assure a Buddhist that he has not changed his culture or nationality, which have to do with where he was born, what he eats, what he wears, and what passport he carries. Those things do not need to change. I tell Buddhists, "The real change takes place inside your heart, the real *you*, the eternal part which nobody else but God can see." When God transforms our hearts, there will be outward evidence such as a supernatural desire to forgive our enemies, to love those who dislike us, to read the Bible, to pray, to be part of a Bible-believing church, and to share the gift of Jesus Christ with others.

## A PRAYER FOR GOD'S POWER

Once a Buddhist gets saved, I tell him straightaway, "I want to leave you with another Gift. I know that when I'm gone, you won't know how to pray to God yet, but the Holy Spirit can help you. Let's pray for you to be filled with the Spirit so you can pray to God supernaturally like the disciples did in Acts chapter 2."

The Bible declares, "They were all filled with the Holy Spirit and began to speak in other tongues (heavenly languages), as the Spirit gave them utterance" (Acts 2:4). I ask a Buddhist background believer, "If you were born to an English-speaking parent, what language would you speak? (English.) If you were born to a Thai parent, what language would you speak? (Thai.) So if you were born of the Spirit, what would you speak? That's right, a Spiritual language! When we are born of the Heavenly Father, we get to speak a Heavenly language!" Weymouth's translation of 1 Corinthians 14:2 explains that when Christians speak in tongues, we are speaking spiritual secrets to God our Father!

We are supernatural children of a supernatural God, we have a supernatural assignment and we face a supernatural enemy. It stands to reason that the Holy Spirit would give us a supernatural way to pray. By praying in tongues, we build up our spirit man (Jude 1:20), pray for God's perfect will (Romans 8:26-27), rest and refresh our souls (Isaiah 28:11-12), and pray for the future or unknown (1 Corinthians 14:2).

One of the most powerful Christians in recent history was the British evangelist Smith Wigglesworth. He was an uneducated man, a plumber by trade. Yet he had revival on every continent he visited and raised over 20 people from the dead. To what did he credit his success? He credited it to someone who told him about the Biblical experience of being filled with the Spirit, and subsequently he practiced praying in tongues two hours every day! Paul, one of the most effective missionaries in Christianity, said, "I thank my God I speak in tongues more than you all" (1 Corinthians 14:18). One cannot overestimate the importance of praying in other tongues in one's prayer life.

Don't let the devil stop you from asking the Father for the infilling of the Spirit. Ask and the Father promised you will receive! Then by faith, begin to speak the first unknown words that come to you. I have seen many receive this joyful experience as they prayed this prayer:

*"Lord, Your Word says that if I ask for the gift of the Holy Spirit, I will receive. I ask You to fill me with the Holy Spirit and enable me to talk to You in my own supernatural prayer language. By faith I will*

*begin to speak in other languages, unknown to my mind, but known
to God. In Jesus' Name, I will begin now."*

Now by faith begin to pray to God in other tongues!

S ince you have accepted God's forgiveness of your sins
through Jesus Christ, He has given you a brand new
spirit, "a spirit that shines like a lightning bug!" The pure
Holy Spirit has come to dwell in you forever. He will never
leave you or forsake you. You will be able to talk to God and
pray in the Spirit every day. What a great privilege He
gave us!

As we continue to feed on God's Word and pray in the
Holy Spirit, we will be able to overcome addictions and
things we disliked about ourselves. I know I did. No religion
changed me. But God took out my old selfish nature and put
His loving nature in my heart. God took out my old desires
for things that did not glorify Him, and put in His new
desires that are clean and holy. I did not try to quit anything
out of fear or condemnation. The Spirit of God empowered
me to walk a new life and gave me opportunities I could
never imagine. For all His love I praise Him!

QUESTION & ANSWER

W hy aren't Buddha's prophecies about the end
times and the Coming Holy One and Buddha's
teachings about karma not more known?

Buddha's teaching on the 5 commandments, the 10
karmas, the 8 levels of Hell, and his parables on the heavy

price of karma and his prophecies of Someone Greater than himself all sound very much like the Old Testament. Buddha really paved the way for sinners to trust in Jesus.

There are probably many reasons why people don't hear more about this, and the intention of this book is to bring about more awareness. Remember the rabbis under the Old Testament had all the evidence to see that Jesus was the fulfillment of their Scriptures, yet politics and religious blindness prevented them from accepting Jesus as the Messiah. It would not be very difficult for the average Buddhist to see the eternal benefits of believing in Jesus Christ for themselves, but those who are in Buddhist leadership may perceive that they have more to lose. They may feel somewhat like the Pharisees who were threatened by Jesus. If they embraced the truth about God, they would in fact not lose anything, but gain everything!

Besides personal reasons, there are also historical factors which explain why Buddha's original teachings have become corrupted and why there exists many disagreements within Buddhism. We will take a look at two of these factors: (1) the splintering denominationalism and (2) the source text of Buddhism itself.

2 3

# WHICH DENOMINATION?

## WHAT DID BUDDHA TEACH?

W hat did Buddha really say? This is actually going to depend on which Buddhist denomination you subscribe to. Buddhism much like Christianity is fragmented into many denominations[1].

Much as Christianity is divided into two[2] main branches, Catholics and Protestants, so too Buddhism is divided into two[3] main ones, Mahayana and Hinayana.

## HINAYANA

Although today there are two main denominations of Buddhism, there were many to start off with. At the time of King Asoka[4] (Thai *Asoke*, English *Without Sorrow*), one of the ancient kings of India, there were actually 18 denominations of Buddhism. All of them are now defunct except one. The only one that survived out of those 18 is called Hinayana[5].

Hinayana is the form of Buddhism prevalent today in Sri Lanka, Cambodia, Laos, Myanmar, and Thailand. We could call it **"Southern Buddhism"**. It's considered the oldest, strictest and purest form of Buddhism. For this reason it is also known as Theravada [6] or the "Way of the Elders."

## MAHAYANA

A newer denomination called Mahayana[7] possibly emerged out of India in the 1$^{st}$ century BC, became a movement in China in the 2$^{nd}$ century, traveled to South Korea and crossed over to Japan[8] by the 6$^{th}$ century. Hence we could call it **"Northern Buddhism"**.

When you examine Mahayana Buddhism, you will see that they are mixing some of the local belief systems with traditional Buddhism. They honor other buddhas in addition to the historical Buddha. They add a mythology of ghosts, gods, goddesses, protecting spirits, and so-called Mahayana saints (Sanskrit: *bodhisattvas*).

The most famous of these saints is Guan Yin.[9] She is worshipped as a saint in a similar way Catholics venerate Mary. Catholics are ambivalent about whether Mary is divine or merely a human being who gave birth to the Savior of the world. Catholics may not say Mary is above Jesus, yet many Catholics venerate her more than they do Jesus. In a similar way Mahayana Buddhists end up venerating Guan Yin more than they do Buddha. They would be ambivalent about whether or not she's a god, yet if they had to pray, they wouldn't pray to Buddha, they would pray to Guan Yin first. A lot of Catholics also won't pray in the Name of Jesus, but they will pray to Mary first.

## THE STORY OF FEMALE WORSHIP

Female worship is a very interesting development in both our religions. Obviously this is not what either Jesus or Buddha intended. The misunderstanding about Christianity runs so deep that many Muslims believe the Trinity refers to "God the Father, Mary the Mother of God, and Jesus" – which concept Muslims violently reject, as do also Christians! When we go back to the Bible, we find that Mary was a special woman indeed, but not once worshipped. No one ever prayed to her. Biblical Christianity gives at least 3 witnesses about Mary:

The angel Gabriel spoke of Mary, "Blessed are you *among* women!" (Luke 1:28). Had he intended to recognize her divine status, Gabriel should have said, "Blessed are you *above* all women!" Gabriel did not.

Mary spoke a psalm of praise when she and her cousin Elizabeth were thanking God for their supernatural pregnancies. Mary sang, "My soul has rejoiced in God *my Savior*" (Luke 1:47). Who needs a Savior but a sinner? Mary acknowledged she was a sinner who needed a Savior just like everybody else. She was not sinless like the Son of God whom she was destined to carry. Jesus alone was sinless and therefore able to save sinners, including Mary.

When one man interrupted Jesus' sermon by drawing attention to the presence of his mother and brothers, Jesus retorted, "Who is My mother and who are My brothers?" And He stretched out His hand toward His disciples and said, "Here are My mother and My brothers! For whoever does the will of My Father in Heaven is My brother and sister and mother" (Matthew 12:47-50). If we believe Jesus, then doing the will of God is more important than paying attention to Mary.

When a woman interrupted Jesus, He had a similar response. Luke 11:27-28 records: "And it happened, as He spoke these things, that a certain woman from the crowd raised her voice and said to Him, 'Blessed is the womb that bore You, and the breasts which nursed You!' But He said, *'More* than that, blessed are those who hear the word of God and keep it!'" What was Jesus saying? Mary was blessed to be chosen by God to carry His Son, but any

Christian who hears God's Word and does it is *more* blessed than Mary!

L astly, we refer once more to Mary's own words. There was only one occasion when someone tried to depend on Mary to intercede for them. This was during the wedding feast of Cana, where they ran out of wine. Someone who did not have a relationship with Jesus approached Mary to inform her of the predicament. Her reply was not, "Let me perform a miracle for you!" Instead her reply was, "Whatever He [Jesus] says to you, do it!" (John 2:5). Mary knew the secret to receiving miracles from God was to obey Jesus. Would that more Christians listened to Mary!

The point here is that praying to Mary was completely foreign to the New Testament and would have shocked the Blessed Virgin herself. The idea of worshipping Mary is nothing more than human invention.

Its followers reason that if we should worship Jesus, how much more should we worship Mary His mother? By logical extension, we should worship even more Ann! Ann, for those who do not know, was Mary's mother! If we continued along this line of human reasoning, how far back should we go? Theoretically we should worship our oldest ancestor Adam, the first sinner. The reason ancestor worship is not in the Bible is our ancestors were all sinners. Only Jesus was born sinless, lived sinless, and died sinless. Jesus is unique. Jesus alone is divine and worthy of worship.

When we speak of Christianity, we do not refer to Mary worship because it was an unscriptural practice added after Jesus rose again and after the Bible was completed. Likewise, when we speak of Buddhism, we do not refer to the worship of Guan Yin because a lot of Mahayana teaching came long after the time of Buddha.

Some may wonder why they sometimes see statues of the

goddess Guan Yin in a Theravada Buddhist temple. Theravada Buddhists are willing to mix their beliefs with Chinese traditions because the Chinese are considered rich. Money buys. These Theravada temples are not strictly following the Theravada way. Follow the money.

## VAJRAYANA

There is a third school of Buddhism I'm only going to mention briefly. It's called Vajrayana.[10] It's the form of Buddhism that exists in Tibet and Mongolia. Shingon Buddhism in Japan is also considered Vajrayana.

Vajrayana, also known as Tantrayana, is more esoteric than the other schools. It's got secret practices. It's got stories which Tibetan monks claim Buddha secretly taught his disciples.

The main distinctive of Vajrayana is that whereas earlier Buddhism implied it would require many merits over many lifetimes to achieve nirvana, Vajrayana claims to provide an accelerated path to enlightenment. One may say Hinayana is the slow track. Vajrayana is the fast track!

The fast track simply means more rules, such as circumambulations of holy sites and mountains, frequent prostrations, and repetition of prayers. The new initiate will not know much about these rules because secrecy is a cornerstone of Tibetan Buddhism. High level lamas are not allowed to share all the rules to the uninitiated, but we are aware that they involve chanting, yoga, the use of bells and drums, and sexual exercises to redirect one's sexual energies towards a greater goal. These practices demand high levels of discipline and a lot of suffering.

A common element of many religions is self-inflicted suffering. This can be found in Tibetan Buddhism, Filipino and Latino forms of Catholicism and Shi'a Islam. Within our conscience, all of us know that we are sinners, and our sins deserved to be punished. Only the sincerest but misguided among us take it a step further by punishing themselves through harsh treatment of their flesh, even self-flagellation. If only they knew that Jesus suffered the sum total of every man's sin once for all, they would be relieved to know that salvation is paid for, and they no longer need to suffer now in this life nor in the next.

## WHICH BUDDHIST DENOMINATION?

After Buddha's death in the 5th century BC, there arose 18 competing schools of Buddhism. Theravada is the only surviving one of those ancient schools. Whereas Chinese Buddhism emerged later in the 2nd century and added new scriptures[11] with new ideas such as the veneration of bodhisattvas[12]; and Tibetan Buddhism emerged later in the 7th century, adding new scriptures[13] with new instructions such as how to prepare the dying; Theravada stayed strictly with the original teachings of Buddha. Therefore it is considered the purest *nikai* or denomination. It ought to be, as far as anyone can tell, closest to what Buddha taught historically.

Therefore it's my understanding that Theravada Buddhism is the oldest and strictest form. It's also my understanding that Thailand is the largest practicing Buddhist country in the world. So for these two reasons we have focused on Buddhism as it is lived and practiced in the largest Theravada Buddhist country in modern times. However, I have not excluded perspectives from other countries when it was appropriate to touch on them.

The above overview of Buddhist denominations was necessary because the reader should understand that whatever I say may not be accepted or agreed upon by all

Buddhist denominations. This will, of course, be the case because there are numerous divisions between themselves. However, we can say that as far as the oldest sect goes, and as far as the largest Buddhist country goes, this is what most Buddhists believe and practice.

## QUESTIONS & ANSWERS

**W**ho is the Dalai Lama?
A noteworthy distinction of Tibetan Buddhism is the Dalai Lama. The term was bestowed by a Mongolian emperor on a Tibetan monk in 1578, and is a mix of Mongolian and Tibetan words.[14] The Dalai Lama used to serve as a priest for the rulers of Mongolia, who first invaded Tibet in 1240. He maintained some political power over Tibet under his various Mongolian and Chinese rulers, but lost it when Tibet fell under communist China. The current Dalai Lama was exiled to India in 1959 and has technically renounced political power, although his sermons remain very nationalist and political.

The belief in a Dalai Lama is the result of mixing influences from Chinese Buddhism and Hinduism. The original Indian version of Buddhism teaches that Sakyamuni Buddha was the 10th reincarnation of a person and because he has become Buddha, he has passed out existence. He has won the privilege to never be reincarnated again, so who is the Dalai Lama?

The Dalai Lama is considered the reincarnation of the male Buddha of Compassion, who is known in China as the female goddess **Guan Yin** (or Lady Mercy), and whose identity may have been borrowed from a Hindu god such as

Shiva or Vishnu. The present Dalai Lama is held to be the 14th reincarnation of this person.

The Dalai Lama will never have any power or influence in a traditional Buddhist country other than Tibet. His existence, in a certain sense, contradicts Buddhism. Tibetan Buddhism teaches that this Buddha is reborn again and again, and evidently always in Tibet. But conservative Buddhism teaches that once someone is enlightened or becomes a Buddha, he passes out of existence completely.

The Dalai Lama is the unique belief from a third form of Buddhism that exists only in Tibet. It is not considered the belief of the original form of Buddhism that existed in India, Sri Lanka, and Southeast Asia.

The present 14th Dalai Lama has repeatedly stated that he will never be reborn inside a territory controlled by the People's Republic of China, and has occasionally suggested that he might choose to be the last Dalai Lama by not being reborn at all! ...Which is just as well because China has recently (Aug 2007) passed a law that bans Buddhist monks in Tibet from reincarnating without government permission.[15]

W hat is Zen?
Zen is a late form of Buddhism that started in 7th century China and spread to Japan. The word "zen" is related to the Sanskrit word *dhyana* which means meditation. Zen emphasizes direct personal experience through meditation. Sacred texts and theoretical knowledge are viewed with skepticism. Zen masters do not attach much importance to words, but rather aim for peace by seeking nothing. Zen rejects a scholarly search of truth, which is ironic considering it is most popular in Western universities.

What do you think about meditation?

Meditation is important to both Buddhists and Christians. Interestingly, most Buddhists do not practice meditation, yet are known for it; while Bible-believing Christians probably practice meditation more than they realize, yet are unknown for it!

I am aware of several experiences of Buddhists and Christians I would like to share, but time and space limits me. Suffice it for me to touch briefly on two issues.

First, the most common misunderstanding of Westerners who meditate is they think they are a *mind*. We have a mind, of course, but we are *not* a mind. The Bible teaches that God made us like Himself, and since He is three in one, we are also three in one. We are made of 3 parts – spirit, soul, and body (1 Thes 5:23, Heb 4:12). The spirit is the real and eternal part of us. It's also called the hidden man of the heart (1 Pet 3:4). When we break up with someone we love, we say we have a "broken-heart". We don't say we have a "broken head," do we?! Because we know we are more than a head, a mind or a collection of hormones.

When you meditate in the Eastern sense, you are not merely emptying your mind. Your spirit can leave your body, and evil spirits can then come in to possess your body. Western psychologists don't believe in the spiritual world so they would say it's a mental problem. Those who don't carefully guard their hearts and minds with the Truth of God's Word are susceptible to demonic oppression or possession. Jesus met a lot of these cases and cured them. Only when the Holy Spirit of God comes to live in you, then no demon is allowed to possess you. Christians are the Temple of God and God doesn't share His home with any evil spirit. I wish more people understood spirit, soul and body.

The second comment I'd like to make is the main difference between mystical and Biblical meditation. One is meditating on nothing, in order to empty one's mind. The second is meditating on something (God's Word), in order to get clarity on a course of action! My wife is very good at Biblical meditation. All believers are commanded to meditate. God said to Joshua, "This Book of the Law shall not depart from your mouth, but you shall meditate in it day and night, that you may observe TO DO according to all that is written in it. For then you will make your way prosperous, and then you will have GOOD SUCCESS" (Joshua 1:8). Biblical meditation is vital to fulfilling God's plan for your life.

# THE THREE BASKETS (TRIPITAKA)

## TRIPITAKA

It is generally accepted that what Buddha taught is recorded in a sacred text called the *Tripitaka* in Sanskrit or *Pra-trai-pidok* in Thai, which means the "three baskets". Why three baskets?

The stories of Buddha were handed down orally until they were recorded on palm leaf scrolls. They had to use a lot of scrolls to write down the 10,000 stories of Buddha, so they organized and kept these scrolls in three different baskets; hence *Pra-trai-pidok*. The 'pra' is simply an honorary prefix, and the 'trai' shares the same root as Trinity, meaning three.

So the roots of all languages obviously go back to Babylon, where the Bible says one proto-language was confounded into many (read Genesis 11).

## LINGUISTICS

While common daily words (such as *hi, bye, welcome, thank you, yes, no,* and *I love you*) may bear no resemblance among foreign languages, key Biblical words nearly always share similar roots in languages all over the world.

The Trinity is a key concept of the Biblical Creator God, and 'tri' is the root word for three in most European and Indian languages (*trois* French, *tres* Spanish, *tre* Italian, *drei* German, *tri* Pali-Sanskrit).

The 7 day week is universally accepted among Buddhists and Christians, yet unlike the day, month or year, the week has no astronomical basis on the movement of the sun, moon, stars or even the earth. The only basis for a 7 day week is God's Story of Creation in Genesis, where God created the universe in 6 days and rested on the 7$^{th}$, calling it the *Sabbath*. The word for the 7 day week in other languages? *Semaine* in French, *semana* Spanish, *sabda* Thai. The universal truth of the Bible is inculcated in every culture that has a 7 day week.

The oldest prediction of a coming Savior who would offer a sacrifice for sin and conquer evil is found in the Book of Genesis, where God promised Adam that the "seed of the woman" (a Person born without a man's sperm) will arrive and reverse the effects of the man's sin and fall. This special messenger has been expected in many cultures which call Him *Mashiach* in Hebrew, *al-Masih* in Arabic, *Messiah* in English, *Maitreya* in Sanskrit, *Metteya* in Pali, *Pra-Med-trai* in Thai, *Miroku* in Japanese, and *Miruk* in Korean. God's promise of hope has been etched in the memory of mankind, no matter what language he speaks.

One of the most important truths from the Bible is the power of calling upon the "Name" of the Lord. When sinful men lost touch with God, their earliest form of worship was by calling upon God's Name. Long before Sikhs or Hare Krishnas adopted the idea of calling on God's Name, the Bible records that from the earliest times, since the third generation from Adam, "Then men began to call on the name of the LORD." (Genesis 4:26) The New Testament instructs us that by calling on the Name of Jesus, anyone can be saved from their sins! "And it shall come to pass that whoever calls on the name of the Lord shall be saved." (Acts 2:21) Peter preached in his first sermon about Jesus, "Nor is there salvation in any other, for there is no other name under heaven given among men by which we must be saved." (Acts 4:12) Is it any surprise that the word for 'name' is one of the most uniform sounds in all languages? *Nom* in French, *nombre* Spanish, *naam* Hindi, *nam* Thai, *nanme* Burmese, *nama* Indonesian, *namae* Japanese. The widespread similarity is hard to miss.

One final interesting parallel.

The patriarchs of the Bible – Abraham, Isaac, and Jacob – knew God by a particular name: *Shaddai*. They lived about 4000 years ago or 500 years before the time of Moses. One of the most ancient cultures in the world – the Chinese – called God by this name: *Shan Ti*. The resemblance is uncanny and obviously adds credence to the fact that the first Chinese who settled in China came from Babel with the knowledge of God Almighty. Later God revealed to Moses, "I appeared to Abraham, to Isaac, and to Jacob, as God Almighty [*El Shaddai*], but by My name, LORD [*Jehovah*], I was not known to them." (Exodus 6:3) The ancients knew Him as *Shaddai* or *Shan Ti*, but the modern believers know Him as *Jehovah* or *Jesus!* Jesus is a Greek form of the Hebrew name *Joshua*, literally "Lord Who Saves!" What a name for the Savior of the world!

To return to our original topic, the *Tripitaka* is the main sacred text of Buddhism. However, just as Muslims depend on the *Hadith* to illuminate the *Koran*, so too Buddhists refer to non-canonical commentaries to shed light on the *Tripitaka*.

To add to the lack of uniformity in Buddhism, there are many versions of the *Tripitaka* – Pali, Sanskrit, Chinese,

Tibetan, Cambodian, Thai, etc. Unlike the Bible, all versions do not refer to the same stories.[1] The Tibetan version contains stories not found elsewhere and secret teachings. The Chinese version is probably the most copious, amounting to 120 times the size of the Bible![2] Compare this to the Pali Canon, which is still a hefty volume, weighing in at 15 times the size of the Bible.[3] The most conservative one is the Pali Canon.

No one is sure when the *Tripitaka* was written. The teachings were first transmitted orally, and then compiled anywhere between 247BC-500AD, which is as late as a thousand years after the time of Buddha! The earliest Thai manuscripts on record date from 1477; but most manuscripts date much later from the 1800s onwards.

Based on the lateness of the Buddhist texts, I suspect that the dominant Hindu religion had plenty of time to reassert its influence on the religion of a Hindu heretic. Buddha did not follow Hinduism or its idols. I question some teachings attributed to Buddha, such as later assertions of his miraculous powers or belief in reincarnation. They sound more like Hinduism amalgamating into Buddhism. They simply don't align with a man searching for a way out of suffering, and rejecting Hinduism as that true way.

It is interesting to note that Westerners rarely question the reliability of Buddha's story, but feel obliged to incessantly discredit the reliability of Jesus' story. Their rejection is not based on facts, but on ignorance or prejudice. In contrast to the *Tripitaka*, all of the New Testament was written by eye witnesses of Christ within 100 years of the events, and the earliest manuscripts on record date from the first century. No other piece of historical literature is as well attested to as the Bible.

## THE THREE BASKETS

The *Tripitaka* contains 40 books (Burmese edition), 45 books (Thai edition), or 57 books (Pali edition) categorized into 3 sections, or literally 3 baskets.

The first basket is about **Discipline**: *Winayan* in Thai or *Vinaya* in Pali. Books 1 to 8 of the Thai edition belong to the *Winai-pidok* (Thai) or *Vinaya-pitaka* (Pali). They contain the rules and laws that a Buddhist needs to keep in order to escape sin and go to Heaven. There are lots and lots of rules and laws to keep. What's interesting is that when Westerners teach about Buddhism as a religion of peace and freedom, they rarely emphasize these rules. The very first and most important part of the *Tripitaka* are the rules. Without following the moral laws you can never escape karma or its consequent suffering.

The second part is about **Doctrine**: *Tamma* in Thai or *Dharma* in Sanskrit, meaning truth or teachings. This section contains the *sutras* or stories of Buddha and his disciples. For this reason it is also known as the *Sutras* (Sanskrit for threads) or *Sutta* (Pali for threads). Buddha taught for about 45 years, and then his disciples continued to teach and recount the stories that he taught. Altogether these form the Buddhist teachings or *tamma*, considered very important. Books 9 to 33 belong to the *Suttata-pidok* (Thai) or *Sutta-pitaka* (Pali).

The third part is a **Commentary** on the Doctrine: *Abhi-tamma* in Thai or *Abhi-dharma* in Sanskrit. The name literally means "beyond the dharma" or "higher tamma". This section attempts to explain, reword and reorganize the stories into a systematic theology. Books 34 to 45 belong to the *Abhi-tamma-pidok* (Thai) or *Abhidhamma-pitaka* (Pali).

The *Abhidharma* was collected hundreds of years after Buddha died. In Sri Lanka and Myanmar the *Abhidharma* is more venerated, however in Thailand it plays a minor role compared to the first two parts. This third section is very dense and difficult to understand. It is a more theoretical and philosophical part of the *Tripitaka*, so most Buddhists never read it. If they do want to know something about it, they might read commentaries on the Commentary.


## COMPARING THE BIBLE WITH THE TRIPITAKA

The Bible and the *Tripitaka* should not be viewed as two competing books. The *Tripitaka* contains the history of one part of the world, India, while the Bible contains the history of another part of the world, Israel.

The subject of the *Tripitaka* is man. The subject of the Bible is God.

The *Tripitaka* is full of instructions for one to be a better person, but does not address questions like where we came from, where we are heading, or what is the purpose of life. The Bible answers all these questions without contradicting the instructions for people to be good. The 10 Commandments of Moses (1500 BC) are repeated in 4 out of 5 moral laws of Buddha (550 BC) and even God's prohibition against idolatry (Moses' 2nd commandment) is repeated elsewhere in Buddha's teachings (Pali: *appa-mano* don't make idols! *a-mita-bucha* don't worship materially!).

The Bible is written in common language and considered every Christian's handbook for salvation. The *Tripitaka* is written in a foreign language or translated into very high archaic language that the average person does not understand. This is being changed as newer editions of the *Tripitaka* are being revised, but apart from a few stories taught to children in schools, the *Tripitaka* will always be considered the domain of monks and scholars. By sheer size of its volume (45 books), the general public will never read it, at least not in the same way a Christian mum, businessman or pastor would pick up the Bible and read it every day. Many Christian families read through the entire Bible together every year! This is completely impractical for the typical Buddhist family.

Lastly, the *Tripitaka* is full of instructions for controlling the flesh. (Even meditation which has a spiritual goal starts out with controlling the flesh. Being a monk means renouncing the flesh, shaving the head, and wearing a robe.) It is working from outside in. The Bible is full of instructions for sinners to repent and believe God from the heart. God works from inside out. This does not contradict the *Tripitaka*. It only works from a different direction. God wants to change our spirits first. Even if you did everything right in the flesh, when you die you would still go to Hell, because your spirit is unsaved. God deals with our nature by replacing it with His own Son's.

## How We Got the Bible & the Tripitaka

There are at least 5 important differences between the history of how the Bible and the *Tripitaka* came to be.

First, the *Tripitaka* was passed down orally, whereas the Bible was quite literally set in stone from the beginning! God wrote the first 10 Commandments on 2 tablets of stone, then instructed Moses to record every word of God and the history of His dealing with the new nation of Israel. From ancient times, Israel was a 100% literate society. Moses was commanded to write[4], parents were commanded to write[5], kings were commanded to write[6], and prophets were commanded to write[7]. The written record of God's Word multiplied rapidly among religious and secular people. In contrast, the *Tripitaka* was committed to memory. For a long time it was required that all monks recite the 227 laws of the *Winai-pidok* every 15 days. Failure to do so meant punishment.

. . .

S econd, when the *Tripitaka* was written, two unique things happened. One, it was written in a language that had no writing system – *Pali*. This meant that Pali had to be transliterated into several Indian and Asian writing systems. Two, the texts were written on palm leaves[8] tied together by a string[9]. They look like a Chinese fan when it's folded up, only larger. There were thousands of these!

In contrast, the Bible was from early on written on papyrus, animal skins, and copper plates. All three examples can be found among the Dead Sea Scrolls which date from 250 BC to 100 AD. In the dry atmosphere of the desert, Biblical texts were very well preserved. In the humid weather of Asia, palm leaves did not survive well. Most of them have rotted. Therefore we no longer have the originals with which to compare the present version of the *Tripitaka*.

T hird, unlike the Bible, the *Tripitaka* was never published in one single volume until the 20th century. Thousands of palm leaves existed before and there is no way to tell if all the palm leaves were faithfully copied and collected into the present *Tripitaka*.

F ourth, unlike the Bible, the *Tripitaka* was not classified into chapters and verses. Any Christian can find a Bible reference by being told its chapter and verse. These are unchanging in every Bible in every language. References to the *Tripitaka* differ greatly depending on which version of the *Tripitaka* a monk was referring to. If he was looking at palm leaves, he might reference them as *pook*[10] *1, 2, 3, etc* or by a story title known to the listener. However, if he was reading from a bound book, he would tell his fellow monks to turn to such page and go to such line. Of course, pages and lines might differ between different editions of the *Tripitaka*. Today, one can find a *Tripitaka* online with clear paragraph numbers, but this is a recent development.

The lack of a single universal classification means two things for us. One, it is not easy to find old references to Buddhist stories. Secondly, there is simply no way to guarantee that every story and every line from the original *Tripitaka* has been faithfully transmitted to the present version.

The Jewish rabbis, on the other hand, knew the exact number of Hebrew letters in the *Torah* (Hebrew for "Law" or the first five books of the Bible). The number of letters in the *Torah* is 304,805. That's how we know the Bible was faithfully transmitted letter by letter and why Bible codes (equi-distant letter codes) are possible. If one letter went missing, any code intentionally placed by the Author would fail. That is, any encoded message would be impossible to decode. But we do find, in fact, many intelligent codes in the Bible, attesting not only to its supernatural origin, but absolutely faithful preservation.

Fifth, unlike the Bible, the *Tripitaka* has undergone many major revisions and corrections. Besides all the minor corrections and updating which may happen as often as every 10 years, there have been overall reviews by Buddhist Councils. The Burmese claim that 6 Councils have met to agree on and revise Buddhist doctrines. Thais claim there were 9 councils in history.

One significant Council for the Thais, usually omitted from the official list, was called by the First King of Thailand[11] in order to salvage the Buddhist texts destroyed in an attack on *Ayutthaya* by the Burmese in 1767.

# THE SIX BUDDHIST COUNCILS

Each Council met to purify doctrine and clean up mistakes, misinterpretations and heresies. The 6 commonly accepted Buddhist Councils were:

**First Council** in 543 BC, three months after Buddha's death.[1] His cousin and favorite disciple Ananda was said to be gifted with a great memory for all of Buddha's sayings. The only concern was that Ananda had not attained buddhahood. Coincidentally, it was announced that Ananda had become enlightened the night before the Council met.

*Ananda and Maha-Gasapa are often depicted on each side of Buddha in Buddha art.*

Maha-Gasapa[2] presided over this Council. Nothing was recorded but the first two parts of the *Tripitaka* were committed to memory.

**Second Council** in 443 BC[3], 100 years after Buddha's death. This resulted in a split in the *sangha* or religious community.

**Third Council** in 250 BC, 293 years after Buddha's death.

King Asoka had gained control of India by killing all of his brothers except one, *Tissa*. King Asoka wanted to deal with the many Buddhist heresies by this time. The first course of action was violent. His minister went down a line of seated monks and beheaded all the "heretics" until he came to *Tissa*. Then it was decided a Council would be better to purge the *sangha* of heretics and purify the *Tripitaka*. When an accepted orthodoxy was agreed upon, it was committed to memory and recited. King Asoka sent missionaries to propagate it all over the known world and even boasted of sending missionaries as far as ancient Greece!

For the person who thinks that Buddhism is not an evangelistic religion, one must ask how Buddhism ever got to the rest of Asia? The Third Council's version of the *Tripitaka* arrived in Sri Lanka and became known as the Pali Canon or "Teaching of the Elders" (Theravada).

**Fourth Council** in 100AD, 643 years after Buddha's death. It was clear by this time that most monks could not recite the entire *Tripitaka*. Meeting in Kashmir, northern India, 449 monks compiled a new canon and wrote it on palm leaves. The canon was composed of mixed beliefs from various Buddhist denominations. This was outrightly rejected by the Theravada school.

Here was a clear demarcation where Theravada and Mahayana began to seriously diverge, the Theravada relying on Pali and the Mahayana on Sanskrit.

**Fifth Council** in 1871, over 2400 years after Buddha's death. The time that had elapsed between the Fourth and Fifth Council was over 1700 years! No such gap can be found in the development of any major religion in the world! The world had changed significantly since 100AD, Western colonization was in full swing and Christianity was impacting the world. Meeting for the first time outside India, in Mandalay, Burma, monks corrected errors in the *Tripitaka* and inscribed the new version on 729 marble stones.

**Sixth Council** from 1954-1956, literally a modern day event! Held in Rangoon, Burma, the Council was intended to coincide with the 2500<sup>th</sup> anniversary of Buddhism, tipping off great celebrations in Burma.

To put it in perspective, if the Bible were to be revised in any major way in the 1950s, it would be an extremely controversial issue. The fact that the *Tripitaka* was revised as recently as modern times means that modern monks had ample opportunity to "clean up" any resemblance between Buddha's words and Jesus'. By the 20<sup>th</sup> century, Christianity was already well known, and it would be easy for anyone to omit parts of the *Tripitaka* that would remind people of Christianity. I am not saying that it was done deliberately. It may have been done out of sincerity to prevent confusion. For this reason it is important to sometimes refer to sources that pre-date 1956.

OUR SOURCE

I am giving you a picture of the Buddhist texts so you know why the information we have to share is still not commonly known, but really needs to be heard all over the world. I know there are many other people who know these truths and are sharing them! We are privileged to be among the first group of people to translate and publish these Buddhist texts that Westerners rarely emphasize when they talk about Buddhism.

## 26

## KING NARESUAN

**O**ne Man in Exchange for the World?
A common question among Buddhists is, "How can one man die for the sins of the whole world?" There are a few stories I like to use to answer this question. Let me give you two.

### THE HOSTAGE NEGOTIATION

I like to make use of this analogy whenever there is news of a hostage crisis. Once some disgruntled Burmese terrorists held some Thai hostages in the Burmese Embassy in Bangkok. Now suppose one of the hostages was very noble and felt compelled to negotiate with the terrorists with the following offer, "You know what, there are 20 hostages here, why don't you just keep me and let the other nineteen go!" what would the terrorists have thought? "Let nineteen go for one of you? What for?! You are no more valuable to us than the rest of the hostages!" Rightly so.

But suppose the Prime Minister of Thailand drove down to the Embassy and offered, "Take me hostage instead, and let the 20 Thai hostages go," would the terrorists have accepted? Most gladly! Because his high status meant he was a more valuable hostage than 20, 50, or even 100 ordinary hostages!

Likewise, when we trust in man to save us, we are putting our trust in a fellow hostage, who is a sinner just like us and of no more value than us! Christ, however, is the spotless Leader of Heaven. Christ is a more valuable hostage to Hell than all humanity put together! They rejoiced when He died on the Cross and descended into Hell! But their joy was short-lived because three days later Jesus resurrected from the dead!

This analogy would work just as well whenever Muslim terrorists hold Jewish soldiers or foreign civilians as hostage. If the Jewish Prime Minister were ever to negotiate with the terrorists and propose a deal, "Take me hostage instead, and let the soldiers and civilians go," the Muslim terrorists would not miss the opportunity, because the life of one Head of State gives them more negotiating leverage than an airplane full of civilians.

Jesus is the Highest Head of State and King of Heaven. God loves His Son more than any parent ever loved their child. God values Christ's one life as more than fair exchange for all sinners. God considers Jesus' time in hell more costly than all labor that has been done by man from the beginning of the world to its end! He is very precious indeed!

## KING NARESUAN

A second analogy is from the true story of Pra-Naresuan[1] the son of Pra-Maha-Thammaracha. When Thailand fought against Burma and lost, Burma took the King's son in exchange for peace. Rather than allowing the whole nation to be enslaved, the Prince gave his life as security for the liberty of the rest of Thai people. Pra-Naresuan then became highly trained in martial arts and military skills under his Burmese guardians, and three years after the Burmese King died, Pra-Naresuan led a victorious revolt against them. He went on to lead many successful military campaigns, helping the Shan State win independence from Burma, capturing Chiang Mai in 1600, and enlarging Siam's borders to its largest extent.

The parallels between Pra-Naresuan and Jesus are unmistakable. Both were kings' sons. Both were given in exchange for others' freedoms. Both eventually conquered their captors and extended their kingdoms. Both were heroes!

The moral of the story is that one life *can* set an entire people free. Jesus gave His sinless life in exchange for the entire world's freedom!

I like to use analogies from Asian history that are useful for Christians to connect with Buddhists. These familiar stories can serve as aid tools for discipling Buddhists. Space limits me to the purpose of this book, which is to understand Buddhism the way it's actually lived and dispel the myths surrounding Buddhism which many Westerners hold. At a later stage, if given the opportunity, I would like to write another book specifically on evangelizing and discipling Buddhists.

## QUESTIONS & ANSWERS

**You have not yet mentioned the Buddhist concept of 'no soul'. How can we evangelize a people who don't believe they have a personal soul that will be conscious after death?**

I have not talked about the concept of "no soul" (Pali *anatta*) or the "five aggregates" (Pali *khandha*) because it is the domain of theory. In practice, no one that I know of believes they have no soul or that they are made up of five aggregates that will disappear when they die. Only monks might study these things. When you evangelize, you needn't worry about them. I have never yet come across this objection from any Buddhist I've met.

Suffice it for me to refer to someone who takes more of an interest in this issue than I do. Scott Noble wrote an interesting piece called *The Buddhist Road Map* in which he shows how believing in *anatta* would lead people to many contradictions: "The doctrine of 'no soul' undermines the entire premise of the...rebirth tales of Sakyamuni Buddha. Without a soul, what is the connecting point from life to life?" and again, "if there is no soul, why does a Buddhist go to such great lengths to be free from rebirth, and why is it said that Sakyamuni proclaimed at the time of his "last" birth that it was his last birth? WHOSE last birth?"[2]

You also have not yet talked about the Eightfold Path—can you tell us anything about it?

Most Buddhists I encounter cannot name the 8-fold path (Thai *Ariya mak pad*), much less are trying to follow the 8-fold path. It is not a practical reality for most Buddhists. A lot of Buddhists are, however, trying to keep the 5 moral precepts (Thai *seen ha*), but even monks fall short of that ideal. We are all guilty sinners who need the Savior.

The 8-fold path can be divided into three parts:
*seen* (moral rules to control speech and action);
*samathi* (meditation exercises to control the body);
*panya* (wisdom to control the mind).

All these controls are impossible to master because of our tendency to stray and get tired of being good (Christianity calls it "sin nature"). How can we speak of mastering *samathi* or having *panya* when we have not even kept the smallest *seen*?

So in sharing my faith, I do not speak of the 8-fold path. However, I do believe in its noble goals. I believe it is God's will for us to keep the *seen*, practice *samathi* and have *panya*, but how can every one achieve this practically speaking?

When I chose to surrender my life to Jesus, He sent His Holy Spirit within me to transform my old nature into His new nature. In an instant, I became a new creation in Christ. My heart was changed. Whereas I was naturally selfish before, I became less selfish and more loving. What had happened? It wasn't my own effort. God's Love was imparted into my nature. The Bible says of Christians, "The love of God has been poured out in our hearts by the Holy Spirit who was given to us" (Romans 5:5). Self-control is also imparted into our nature. "The fruit of the Spirit is love, joy, peace, longsuffering, kindness, goodness, faithfulness, gentleness, self-control..." (Galatians 5:22-23).

You see, God starts His work inside us – in our spirits – then as we read the Bible and obey it, our minds and bodies also become conformed into the image of Christ. As we allow God to work in us, He will enable us to live morally, meditate prayerfully, and exhibit godly wisdom beyond our years.

The 8-fold path attempts to attain these lofty goals from the outside in – by starting first with controlling the flesh and the mind, but never touching the broken heart or solving the problem of secret sins. God starts with the real us – "the hidden man of the heart" (1 Peter 3:4) – then works His way out. This is practical for everyone.

There are undoubtedly many other things I have not touched on about Buddhism. If one of those things happen to be your interest, please forgive me. My aim is to talk about the things that relate most to **man's greatest need**, which is *salvation from sin* or *deliverance from karma*. For the purposes of witnessing, there is no need for a Christian to get so deep into the theoretical teachings of Buddhism. Buddhists tend to be practical.

Jesus Christ, thank God, is also very practical. Perhaps that's why He as a human chose such a practical trade like carpentry, instead of meditation.

# SUMMARY

## PUTTING IT ALL TOGETHER

Buddha said for one mental sin (*mano-gum*), King Asoka's father had to be reborn an indefinite number of lifetimes – as many times as there are scales on a snake.

Jesus being more precise gave us the exact debt sinners owe in the parable of the *King and the Ungrateful Debtor*. God as the Creditor King has given to every man light, air, food, water, breath, heartbeat, resources, relationships, and opportunities to use and enjoy. Man uses his breath to lie, his heart to lust, other's resources to steal, relationships to benefit self, and opportunities to promote self. By sinning, man owes God 10,000 talents – a spiritual debt he can never afford to pay.

We learned that 1 talent equals 6000 denarii which equals 6000 days' worth of wages. Therefore 10,000 talents equal 60 million denarii, which is 60 million days' or 1,644 lives' worth of perfect works.

If you are a sinner, you are in a pickle because you probably have less than 15,000 days left to live (about 50 years), with no guarantee of tomorrow. Besides that, there have only been 2.2 million days (approximately 6000 years[1]) since the Creation of the first man!

So God looked down from Heaven and saw that no man could pay off humanity's karmic debt. Every man was a debtor. Every man had *gilead tanha* or a sin nature. So God had compassion and came down Himself to pay for man's sins!

In order to be legally punished for mankind, God needed to become a man by having a human body. He did this by stripping Himself of His mighty power and glory (Philippians 2:7), borrowing the Virgin Mary's womb[2] and arriving on earth as a baby in Bethlehem[3]. Being the Owner of the Universe, God's Son was more valuable than the whole universe!

Just as Pra-Naresuan, the King's son, was able to give his life in exchange for all Thai people's freedom, so too God's Son was able to give His life in exchange for all of humanity's freedom. Because of the King's sacrifice, we do not have to fear Satan, death or Hell any more! All we need to do is repent, believe Jesus and be thankful every day for His costly sacrifice for our liberty! Jesus paid the highest price for our salvation!

Do you know that if you would explain the Gospel in this way to Buddhists, many would raise their hands and humbly say, "I am grateful for what Jesus has done for me!" Because they know Buddha taught the right thing, but Buddha could never pay for their sins. When people understand how selfless Jesus is, they will never want to leave Jesus.

When Jesus is presented as the solution to karma and *tukka* (suffering that results from karma), many Buddhists will realize, "If I don't allow Jesus to pay for my karma, I will have to pay for it. If I could be reincarnated, I would still owe at least 1,644 lives for every sin, according to the Lord Jesus. My problem is, every time I come back, I sin some more. It's a vicious cycle of sin and condemnation." Thank God there is hope in Christ Jesus!

What if Jesus had decided not to die for sinners? Then 100% of sinners would go to Hell. I shudder at the thought. I know I could have been one of them. I am so grateful Jesus decided to die for my sins. Are you grateful for His voluntary sacrifice? He did it for you. You are so valuable to God. Yes, God loves you very much.

## QUESTION & ANSWER

How should I witness to someone who believes in reincarnation?

There is no point arguing about reincarnation because: (1) there's no evidence for it, and (2) it only delays the question, "How and when will I get out of my suffering?" True Buddhists want to be rid of karma and end reincarnation. If suffering is the problem of life, then reincarnation isn't the solution, it's merely extending the problem!

I recommend taking them through the moral laws to reveal whether or not they are good enough to go to Heaven, then illustrating the heavy price of sin through Buddha's stories of *King Asoka & the Python*, *The Blind Turtle* or *The Angel and the Stone*.

A friend of mine used what I taught to engage a Sri Lankan Buddhist about her spiritual condition. This is what he said.

I met a woman who was a Sri Lankan Buddhist. She was not very open to God. I asked her if she thought she was a good person. She thought she was. I asked if she kept all the commandments of Buddha. She wasn't sure. So I asked her, "Have you ever lied? Have you ever stolen? Have you ever hated anybody?" Each time she said yes but she would excuse her sin.

She said, "Sometimes I might have to lie to get out of trouble."

"So you're telling me that you only lie when you have to get out of trouble? Are you telling me that you've never lied *in the last week* to suit your own benefit?"

She thought about it and laughed, "Yeah, I probably have lied this week to suit myself."

I quoted James 2:10 to her, "God said, If you break one of My commandments, it's like breaking them all. What do you think will happen to you when you face God on the Day of Judgment?"

She said, "Yeah, I know, but I believe in reincarnation. I'm coming back as another life form."

"As a Buddhist, your goal should be to escape the circle of sin, because that's what Buddha's goal was. If you say you're Buddhist, then you should follow Buddha!" I asked if she knew the story of the Blind Turtle. "Buddha said karma is impossible to erase. Buddha once told us to imagine dropping a yoke into a river and letting it float downstream for three years, then letting a blind turtle try to find it. The day the blind turtle finds that yoke is the day you will be free from your sins! Buddha said your karma gets accumulated every life time, so you will always be in karma."

"What if I like it?" she said, "What if I like to keep on living in karma?"

"If you live in karma, when you die, you're going to be punished, because God said I will punish every sin."

"I'm going to be reincarnated, so it's not going to make any difference." She acted as if she didn't care about her eternal destiny.

I told her, "Think of two situations: first, you're right and

I'm wrong; second, I'm right and you're wrong. Now if *you're right*, you'll die and live another life. I'll die and live another life. We'll both benefit. But what if *I'm right* and you're wrong? Then I'll be in Heaven with Jesus after I die, but after you die where will you be?"

All she could say was, "You have a good point!"

I ended the conversation this way, "Always remember you have two options: (1) dying and finding out there isn't a God, and (2) dying and finding out there is a God and going to Hell."

If there is one chance in a million that there is a Creator God, you owe it to your good sense to find out who the Creator is before you die. He is not far from you. He loves you. He has sent His Word so you can get to know Him. Call on Him to reveal Himself to you, read His Word (especially the New Testament), and you will find you can have a personal relationship with Him.

# 28

# END TIME PREDICTIONS OF
# BUDDHA & JESUS

## THE PURSUIT OF HAPPINESS

Westerners talk about Buddhism as if it's about personal happiness, finding peace within oneself, or freeing one's mind. All that sounds like Buddhism, but it isn't.

I've read claims by Westerners who are trying to practice Buddhism that Buddha said one day Buddhism will bring world peace. In other words, if everyone became Buddhist, the result would be world peace. Nothing of the sort can be found in the *Tripitaka*.

Here is one of Buddha's predictions[1]. It is Buddha's prophecy of the deterioration of truth:

*"Buddha revealed to Pra-Maha-Gasapa Tayra, "Behold, Gasapa, the teaching of morals[2] will slowly and gradually deteriorate. Just as the quality of food deteriorates little by little, year by year, and people do not notice, so too will they not notice when the teaching of truth deteriorates."*

This is similar to what Jesus teaches in the "Kingdom Parables". In Matthew chapter 13 Jesus gives seven parables that describe the Kingdom of God. Some people misinterpret the Seven Kingdom Parables and think they are about how Christianity will become bigger and bigger until the whole world becomes Christian. But Jesus, as a Jewish rabbi, paints a different picture.

He says in one story, "The kingdom of heaven is like leaven" (Matthew 13:33). Any Jewish listener recognizes, "Oh-oh, that doesn't sound so good. The story is already sounding bad," because leaven is a Jewish symbol of sin and corruption. Jesus continues, "Which [leaven] a woman took and hid in three measures of meal till it was all leavened." In other words, the leaven seeped through and corrupted the whole lump of dough. It's painting a picture of the Kingdom of God on earth: it starts out with truth but then false doctrines get inserted in, along with immoral practices, sins, lack of discipline, disrespect for authority, and whatever other things represented by leaven.

Older preachers I know have observed that one of the differences between believers of today and those of previous generations is the modern believers' general lack of commitment. Jesus predicted such a careless state of His church 2000 years ago. Jesus said the church will progressively deteriorate to the point that when He returns, He will ask, "Will I find faith on the earth?" (Luke 18:8). He says brother will turn against brother, father against sons, people will be delivering up their own families to court and to death.[3] That's the message of Jesus' Kingdom Parables: **Left to ourselves, we will never reach perfection, but always corruption.**

Jesus says in another parable, "The kingdom of heaven is like a mustard seed, which a man took and sowed in his field, which indeed is the least of all the seeds; but when it is grown it is greater than the herbs and becomes a tree..." (Matthew 13:31). Anyone in Israel listening to Jesus has to say, "Oh-oh, You are talking about an abnormality of nature. There is no mustard plant that is as big as a tree! A mustard plant is a shrub that you can walk through. It's yellow and small, it's just an herb."

Jesus teaches us that the kingdom of God will grow abnormally large until "the birds of the air come and nest in its branches." Now the Gentile Christian says, "Wow, that sounds great!" Many Gentile preachers get excited and proclaim, "The church is going to overtake the world and it will be awesome! Even birds will come and find rest in the shade of the branches." But we must let the Bible interpret its own idioms. What do the "birds" here refer to? In the first parable describing a sower and four soils, the birds refer to Satan and his demons (Matthew 13:4,19).

The Bible says that Jesus predicts the truth will become so corrupted in the End Times, devils and demons will be attending some churches. There will be false doctrines preached from the pulpit. Are we seeing that today? Are we now seeing some churches taking votes on whether they should ordain a homosexual as pastor? Should they not be consulting the Word of God and obeying the Spirit of God? How far have we strayed from God's ideal for us. **Left to ourselves, we will never reach perfection, but always corruption.**

I am not at all fatalistic about my faith. I believe those who believe will "go from strength to strength" (Psalm 84:7) and "those who know their God shall be strong and carry out great exploits" (Daniel 11:32). But if we are approaching or are in fact already in the *Laodicean* age (symbolized by the last of the seven churches of Revelation), we must be on special guard against pride of denomination and walk in Christian love. How we need to be devoted to God's Word every day.

What kind of picture does the rest of the Bible paint about the end of the age? Is it one of the church overtaking the world? Will everyone be flocking to hear and practice the truth? Will the church at large stand uncompromised? This is what the Holy Spirit says:

## 1 TIMOTHY 4:1 (KJV)

1 Now the Spirit expressly says that in the latter times some shall DEPART from the faith, giving heed to seducing spirits, and doctrines of devils.

O, don't be surprised if the Bible says some will voluntarily leave their faith, don't be surprised! In the latter times some are not going to have to be forced, some are going to voluntarily leave! It won't be the Antichrist threatening them to "renounce Jesus or I'll put a bullet to your head." It will be more like one fine day, the churchgoer who did not ground his faith solidly in the Word of God will think to himself, "I no longer want to be restricted by church and faith, I no longer want to be committed to my brothers and sisters, I want to do what I want to do!"

My point is this: Western humanism paints a picture that people can create peace, clean up the environment, cure diseases, and defeat poverty, all without God and without Jesus Christ. Evidence contradicts this theory. Evidence shows more and worse wars, more and worse pollution, more and worse diseases, and more and worse injustices. This is the deterioration of truth. I am very positive about the future of Bible believers. I believe some of the best preachers, teachers, and churches exist all over the world today! I believe the best is yet to come! But the world at large is about to see terrible days ahead because of its rejection of the truth. Buddha's prediction was not so far off from what Jesus teaches us about the End Times.

Jesus says over and over that when He comes back He will find the world in a state of unpreparedness. So what should we be doing? We should have our lamps burning and our oil topped up. Keep your spiritual fire on for the Lord! Keep your heart burning with passion for Jesus! Keep praying and seeking God in public and in your closet. Remember to keep your heart on the job because the temptation to be complacent and indifferent will be at its greatest as the

Second Coming draws near. Many people will fall away and many will believe only what they want to hear - it's called "itching ears."

**2 TIMOTHY 4:3-5**

**3 For the time will come when they will not endure sound doctrine, but according to their own desires, because they have ITCHING EARS, they will heap up for themselves teachers;**

**4 and they will TURN their ears AWAY FROM THE TRUTH, and be turned aside to fables.**

**5 BUT YOU be watchful in all things, endure afflictions, do the work of an evangelist, fulfill your ministry.**

Mankind needs help. When left without an instructor, man is generally not good at anything - reading, writing, swimming, swinging a golf club, being polite, much less acting morally and developing spiritually. As mankind fulfills the prophecy of "itching ears," desiring less and less to follow God's Word, the world will sink into a time of turmoil. Rather than an increase of peace, which humanism promises, the world will experience an increase of family breakdown, health crisis, financial debt, social rebellion, and natural upheaval (earthquakes, tsunamis, solar flares, meteor impacts). There will be no peace until the Prince of Peace - Jesus Christ - returns to establish peace on the earth.

Buddha agreed with this End Times scenario. Buddha defined the timeline of the Deterioration as follows:

*"When the Buddhist religion is 1,000 years old, there will be no monk who has penetrating insight.*[4]

*When the Buddhist religion is 2,000 year old, there will be no monk who can fly or walk on air*[5]. *People will turn to the **worship of idols**, spirit ghosts and devils.*[6] *This is **a delusion**[7] **that will cause people to fall and go to Hell**.*

*When the Buddhist religion is 3,000 year old, there will be no wisdom among men and the earth will be hot like fire.*[8]

*When the Buddhist religion is 5,000 year old, there will be no monk who can reach the highest level of priesthood. The world will be destroyed by fire[9]."*

It is fascinating how often Buddha and the Bible sound similar. The destruction of the world by fire is also predicted in the Bible. However, the timeline of the Bible puts the end sooner.[10]

### 2 PETER 3:7-12

7 But the heavens and the earth which are now preserved by the same word, are RESERVED FOR FIRE until the DAY OF JUDGMENT and PERDITION of ungodly men.

8 But, beloved, do not forget this one thing, that with the Lord one day is as a thousand years, and a thousand years as one day.

9 The Lord is not slack concerning His promise, as some count slackness, but is longsuffering toward us, not willing that any should perish but that ALL SHOULD COME TO REPENTANCE.

10 But the day of the Lord will come as a thief in the night, in which the heavens will pass away with a great noise, and the elements will MELT with FERVENT HEAT; both the earth and the works that are in it will be BURNED UP.

11 Therefore, since all these things will be DISSOLVED, what manner of persons ought you to be in holy conduct and godliness,

12 looking for and hastening the coming of the day of God, because of which the heavens will be DISSOLVED, being ON FIRE, and the elements will MELT with FERVENT HEAT?

Buddha named the five stages of the Deterioration (in Pali):

*Pa-ri-yat-ti-tam untaratarn* – the deterioration of moral teaching (Thai: *tamma*, Pali: *dhamma*, Sanskrit: *dharma*).

*Pa-ti-bat untaratarn* - the deterioration of moral practice.

*Pa-ti-wade untaratarn* – the deterioration of enlightened thinking or the right way to obtain good results.

*Sangka untaratarn* - the deterioration of the monkhood.

*Untaratarn* - the deterioration of the bones of Buddha.

The Buddhist and Biblical predictions of the deterioration of morals and physical matter[11] are important to us for at least three reasons.

First, it was not obvious to everybody else. What is surprising is that most cultures throughout history did not teach their children this observable process of Deterioration, but rather taught them to believe that man could create his own Utopia. The ancient Chinese Taoists searched for the Elixir of Life, a potion to keep humans young forever, basically trying to defy the Second Law of Thermodynamics. (Entropy states that the universe is moving from a state of order to a state of disorder.) Young Charles Darwin thought lifeless things could beget life[12], plants could beget animals, fish could beget reptiles, reptiles could beget birds, monkeys could beget humans, whereas all evidence shows we are constantly losing old species (as entropy predicts) and not gaining *any* new ones (as evolutionists should expect).

If evolution were true, why should anyone care about extinction? Old species should be disappearing all throughout evolutionary history; while new species should be appearing on a regular basis! Christians care about the extinction of species because no new ones will appear! "A righteous man regards the life of his animal" (Proverbs 12:10). The observable fact is we are not gaining ANY more new species since they were first created!

God said every plant and animal will reproduce "after its own kind". In other words, "like begets like," microbes beget microbes, elephants beget elephants, humans beget humans, and elephants will never beget humans. Unfortunately Darwin did not have the benefit of understanding modern physics because he was formulating his ideas[13] on biology at the same time as physicists were arriving at the Laws of Thermodynamics in the 1850s.

Scientists have recently caught up with the fact that in our fallen world, entropy is law. Buddha spoke of entropy over two millennia ago and the Bible spoke of it in detail over three millennia ago! The wisdom of God may seem foolish to the world but "wisdom is justified by all her children" (Luke 7:35).

Second, the prediction of Deterioration contradicts modern secular assumptions. The world believes that apart from God, we can make our own future bright. World War II was supposed to be "the war to end all wars." The United Nations was to bring peace to the Middle East and stop dictators. The World Health Organization was to eradicate all diseases. How has this modern wisdom done so far? It seems that we should be heeding God's wisdom instead! We keep trying to build our Towers of Babel to reach Heaven by ourselves! All human effort to reach Utopia without God is based on human pride rather than godly humility, and is bound to end in confusion and division.

The Good News is God wants us to succeed. Humility and faith towards God's Word are the keys to success. God said, "Beloved, I wish above all things that thou mayest prosper and be in health, even as thy soul prospereth" (3 John 1:2 KJV). Here's how, "This Book of the Law shall not depart from your mouth, but you shall meditate in it day and night, that you may observe to do according to all that is written in it. For then you will make your way PROPSEROUS, and then you will have GOOD SUCCESS" (Joshua 1:8). I found this to be true in my own life: the harder I try on my own, the more time I waste. But the more time I spend in God's Word, the more time I save and the greater success I find.

My third observation about the End Times predictions of

Buddha and Jesus is that they contradict Western assumption about Buddhism. Westerners assume Buddhism is about peace. I want to correct this common misconception. Neither Buddha nor Jesus predicted peace and happiness in the End Times, but a deterioration of peace and happiness, especially for everyone who has karma and sin, and refuses to repent.

Buddhism is certainly not about Buddha bringing world peace to the earth. Buddhism is not about the goal of achieving personal happiness. Buddha did not teach this. This is Western humanism hijacking Buddhism.

W hat is Buddhism really about?
        The goal of Buddhism is summarized in two words in Thai: *pon tuk*. They mean to be set free from the horrible consequences of sin, or literally, "escape suffering". The cycle of suffering is called *gongjak chiwit*: this is what Buddhism is concerned about!

Buddhism is about finding the way to be free from the vicious cycle of suffering. These two statements may sound similar: 'I want to be free from sin' and 'I want to find happiness,' but they're not aiming for the same goals. Buddha was concerned about being free from the consequences of sin. His heart and mind were focused on the biggest problem that will ruin our future, not on pursuing "what makes me feel happy today."

If Buddhism were about earthly happiness, I can tell you that Siddhartha Gautama was already quite happy as a young man. He had everything most people could ever dream of. How would you feel if you were born a prince with three different palaces for each of the three seasons, you were given a wife at the tender age of sixteen, and you had not a care in the world? If Buddhism was about happiness, Siddhartha would have stayed in his royal palaces!

It's necessary to make this clear because Westerners do not teach nor reveal this about Buddhism. Here's why I think they probably never will. Many Westerners who did not grow up with Buddhism, but take an interest in it later in life, tend to embrace Buddhism as an alternative to Christianity. Buddhism is a way of saying, "I didn't like the church my parents belonged to, I didn't like the boring services I was forced to attend, and now I reject that, so I'm embracing something that's called Buddhism instead," without fully knowing what Buddhism is. They never actually studied Buddhism deeply enough to understand that Buddhism is probably more like Christianity than any other religion in the world! Buddha would have agreed with much of the Old Testament and embraced the gift of the New Testament. If Buddha were alive today, I am convinced he would be in church and love hearing the Good News of Jesus Christ.

Contrary to the popular Western view of Buddhism, personal happiness was certainly not a goal of Buddha. Buddha was concerned with one thing: suffering (Thai: *tuk*, Pali: *tukka*). What was the cause of suffering? Karma, which is sin. He searched all his life to find the way out of sin. Doesn't that sound a lot like Christianity? Only Buddha never found the solution, he never came to a stage where he said, "I've got it, do this and you'll be free from karma." In Christianity we are given the greatest promise by Jesus, "Believe in Me and I will give you eternal life" (John 3:36). A solution is given through Christ's costly blood sacrifice to stop karmic revenge.

# PART II
# CHRISTIAN QUESTIONS

# 29

# THE AUTHORITY OF THE BIBLE

**C**an we quote the Bible to Buddhists?
The Bible (or *Pra Kam Phe* in Thai) is the Holy Book of Christianity, not of Buddhism, yet it is appropriate for Christians to quote the Bible to Buddhists.

Firstly, the truth of God's moral laws have been written on every person's heart. In Romans 2:14-15 the Apostle Paul said, "For when Gentiles, who do not have the law, by nature do the things in the law, these... show the work of the law WRITTEN IN THEIR HEARTS, their CONSCIENCE also bearing witness." When you ask, "Did you know it's wrong to murder? It's wrong to commit adultery?" no Buddhist will disagree.

Secondly, Christians should quote the Bible because the Holy Spirit was sent to testify of Jesus and confirm His Word. The very last verse of the Gospel of Mark says, "And they [the believers] went forth, and preached everywhere, the Lord working with them, and CONFIRMING the WORD with signs following. Amen" (16:20). If we do not speak God's Word, there is nothing for the Holy Spirit to confirm.

Thirdly, Buddhism doesn't have a *Pra Kam Phe* (Bible). Buddhists have a *Tripitaka*, which is not a single book, but a collection of 45 books. It is a massive volume of teachings which we do not know who wrote, which have had at least 6 major revisions, and which most Buddhists have never read. Even most monks have not gone through it in its entirety. The Bible is one concise library of 66 short books, the most concentrated wisdom of the ages, and the most translated and distributed book on earth. So the Bible is a well recognized source of authority.

It would behoove everyone to study the Bible and think for themselves. In contrast to the media's image of the Bible, its account of origins, history, archaeology, politics, science and life has proven true to the unbiased and helpful to millions. Those who believe the Bible have freed slaves, built hospitals, run schools, helped the poor, fed the hungry, visited the imprisoned, invented new technologies, and established the only nations that millions want to migrate to.

W hat about Westerners going on missions to build relationships instead of 'Bible bashing'?

Great question! Should Westerners go to Buddhist countries to develop relationships with people rather than beat them over the head with the Bible?

If by "developing relationships" you mean open conversations with Buddhists, then certainly that is the preferable way to build bridges. In fact, you may have an advantage. People in Developing countries tend to be interested in listening to Westerners. Between you and me, they'd rather listen to you. That's why Asian Pastors are reading Western Christian books. They don't want to read a Thai Christian book. They don't want to study revelation from a Thai. They respect the *farang*.[1] As the world globalizes, this advantage of the *farang* will diminish.

If by "developing relationships" you mean going out cycling together, having tea and coffee, hanging out casually and waiting until they ask you something about Christ, you should first consider a few things.

One, you're going to be in a totally different culture. Country golfing or tea and coffee may not be the way your Buddhist friend socializes. It may work in the West, but it's not the same in Buddhist countries.

Two, the thought of asking you about your faith may never come up, no matter how nice they may think you are.

Three, depending on the length of your stay, you may not have enough time. How much time will you have to build relationships by doing the things that you're used to doing in the West, and still have an opportunity to share the Gospel?

I can build a relationship with someone in 5 minutes. You can, too! How? The friendliest people in the world ask sincere questions and listen. That's it. Learn to ask questions. Don't be so nervous, trying to memorize formulas on how to evangelize or trying to copy someone else you heard. Just a simple, "Hi, how are you?" might be a good start. I don't have a pet question. I try to listen to the Holy Spirit. Whatever the situation is, the Holy Spirit will lead you. Ask the right questions and within 5 minutes the conversation will tend to yield an opening for spiritual matters.

The one thing I have consistently found on every trip to Thailand is that every Buddhist person is suffering. They are suffering in ways that are hard for Westerners to imagine.

In Australia, there is adultery. In Thailand, there are women married to a Thai man and a white man at the same time, and the white man will never know she's using him for money. We don't have such things here in Australia, or at least not as common.

In Australia, we have sexual perverts strolling around schools. In Thailand, the adult picking up children at school may be a parent or a poser who is having an affair with a minor. Some of the minors consent to this relationship because they have a bad family life and can get some love and money. This is not often talked about, and not easy to spot.

In Australia, we have homosexuals. In Thailand, you may not be able to tell who's straight, gay or transvestite. There's no way in two weeks or even two years that you are going to understand this culture.

The best thing you can do is present Christ and let God be God! He understands the Buddhist heart and the Buddhist's needs better than anyone. All you need to understand is that people without Christ are suffering. If you will introduce them to Jesus in a culturally respectful way, they will know whether Jesus has the answer for them or not. They don't need the tea and coffee. They probably won't ride bicycles with you because it's too polluted in many Asian cities. They just need Jesus. Jesus can heal their broken hearts, restore their families, do a miracle in their bodies, and fix their financial troubles. That's what they need and that's what Jesus can do. Most of all, Jesus can forgive their sins and give them eternal life. He just needs someone like *you* to tell them that Jesus loves Buddhists, too.

# 30

# THE VALIDITY OF BUDDHIST STORIES

How reliable are Buddhist texts? I have heard that Buddha's prophecy of a coming Savior is a Christian fabrication.

When one realizes that there have been six to nine Buddhist Councils that have revised and "purified" Buddhist doctrines, the last one occurring as recently as 1956, then one can see the value of sometimes referring to Buddhist sources that pre-date 1956. One former monk named *Tongsuk Siriruk* has greatly helped this effort by writing about the *Tripitaka* in 1954, at least 2 years before the most recent Buddhist Council.

He is a source of some controversy, mainly because his critics cannot find some of his texts in the current *Tripitaka*. They claim that he was a zealous Christian who doctored the texts to promote Christianity. I will reserve my comments in the Appendix as this is a specialized issue not everyone may be equally interested in.

I believe preaching the Gospel is the only way to help people. Why should I care about any non-Christian teaching?

After my own personal search for truth and my experience with the power of Christ, I also believe that the

Gospel is the only answer for mankind. So why do I care about teachings from non-Christian sources?

God is a great God and it shouldn't surprise us Christians if He has left Himself a witness in non-Christian cultures. The *Karen* tribe in Myanmar turned to Christ *en masse* because their tradition taught them that missionaries would bring a book that would tell them about how to be saved from sin.

I heard a similar story of an Ethiopian tribe who turned to Christ because one of their elders told the people to look for someone coming with "gold foils". When a Christian missionary turned up with nothing in his hand but a Bible (whose pages are edged with gold foils), they recognized he was the one who was supposed to bring them Good News!

God said in Isaiah 45:3, "I will give you the treasures of darkness and hidden riches of secret places, that you may know that I, the LORD, who call you by your name, am the God of Israel." Christians may consider Buddhist countries dark and the *Tripitaka* a secret not to be touched, but can't God leave some treasures in the darkness and hidden riches in the secret places, as He promised in the Old Testament?

God told His preacher Jeremiah, "If you take out the precious from the vile, you shall be as My mouth" (15:19). Those who would be God's spokespeople are commanded to take the precious from the vile, not to criticize that 'this religion is vile' and 'that tradition is vile'. We are to look for the positives in the midst of negatives. We are to search for gems of truth that remain in humanity's traditions, and dig out nuggets of life in non-Christian cultures. This is not to replace the preaching of the Gospel, but to prepare people's hearts to hear the Gospel in a culturally relevant way. The Gospel is the answer to every broken heart, the relief of every hurting conscience, the fulfillment of every true longing of every religion.

Our call is not to preach against Buddhism, or teach comparative religions, but to tap into the ally that already exists in every human conscience and some traditions. People may not yet know Christ, but it doesn't mean God hasn't been dealing in their lives. Even of the people who do not yet know God, Solomon said, "He has put Eternity in their hearts" (Ecclesiastes 3:11).

The most hostile criticism that I have seen have not come from Buddhists, who tend to be gentle and non-argumentative about religion, but strangely enough from Christians, some of whom sound very anti-Buddhist. These Christians argue that nowhere in the Bible are we told to quote people outside the Bible.

I think they may need to study the New Testament more carefully. Paul quoted Epiminedes, a Greek philosopher, when he preached his great sermon in Athens, "For in Him we live and move and have our being, as also some of your own poets have said, for we are also his offspring" (Acts 17:28-29). When Paul wrote to Titus who was leading a church in Crete, he quoted a pagan writer named Aratus who was a native of Crete, "One of them, a prophet of their own, said, 'Cretans are always liars, evil beasts and lazy gluttons'" (Titus 1:12-13). Paul was not anti-Epiminedes or anti-Aratus; Paul was pro-Gospel and pro-local culture. We are not to be anti-Buddha or anti-Buddhism, but pro-Jesus and pro-local culture. There is nothing unbiblical about using local wisdom to communicate a point about God. If we look hard enough, I believe we will find that God has left some truth pointing towards His Son in every culture.

# THE RISK OF SYNCRETISM

Isn't there a danger of mixing religions by building bridges to Buddhism?

The danger which some Christians fear is that "building bridges to Buddhists" will result in "syncretism" or the unintended combining or compromising of two religions. Certainly syncretism has happened in the past and is undesirable.

The far worse danger I see, though, is that the Christian Church has struggled to evangelize the Buddhist world for 2000 years, while during the same period of time Buddhism has become more popular in the West. By staying the same course, I believe Christianity is losing ground.

The argument against quoting Buddha seems to go like this: if we quote *one* prophecy of Buddha, we are putting our stamp of approval on *all* words of Buddha. I think this is illogical. Paul certainly did not say *everything* Epiminedes or Aratus said was right. Paul only quoted one of their thoughts as a springboard for dialogue.

Let me digress for a moment to make my point. Chinese Christians have known for some time that certain ancient Chinese characters point back to the story of Genesis. They use this as a springboard for dialogue with non-Christians. For instance, the character for "covet" (to desire something forbidden) is a pictograph of "two trees" and "one woman" under it. What else could this be referring to but Eve considering the fruit of the Tree of Life and that of the Tree of the Knowledge of Good and Evil? There are many such characters in ancient Chinese characters. What Christians are saying is that the earliest Chinese who invented this writing system must have known the account of Genesis. In other words, the first Chinese were believers in God! What Christians are not saying is that *all* Chinese characters point to God or are Biblical!

By quoting Buddha, we are not conceding that everything recorded about Buddha is inspired. We are simply trying to springboard a conversation into the greatest search in life – the search for truth and freedom. We are using what is familiar to the ears of our Buddhist friends and re-loading it with Christian meaning. Christianity used to do this well.

Greek words like *agape* (divine love) and *euanggelion* (from which we get 'evangelism' and 'good news') were adopted from local context and infused with new Christian meaning. Alan Johnson argues in favor of contextualizing the Christian message by using local terms and concepts and investing them with new and higher meanings.[1]

Take Christmas for another instance. The 25th of December 1AD is almost certainly *not* Jesus' birthday. It was more likely in September or October[2]. Yet Christians have taken a pagan holiday celebrating the Winter Solstice and re-loaded it with a Christian meaning. I don't think Christians have suffered too much by celebrating Christmas in December, and probably a lot of good has come out of celebrating Christ instead of the pagan sun god "Yule". Those Christians who oppose Christmas should have the liberty to do so, but should also realize they are aligning themselves with the cult of Jehovah Witnesses, who refuse to celebrate

Jesus' birthday (or any birthday for that matter). I'd rather take every opportunity to glorify Christ.

Easter is another holiday whose influence is probably pagan. Easter bunnies, Easter eggs, and the word "Easter" do not appear in the original language of the Bible. Easter was probably derived from *Astarte* or *Ashtaroth*, the wife of Baal and the 'queen of Heaven'. To be Scriptural, "Easter" should be called "Resurrection Sunday" and should coincide with the Jewish Feast of Firstfruits which typify Christ the First Person to rise from the dead. *"But now Christ is risen from the dead, and has become the firstfruits of those who have fallen asleep"* (1 Cor 15:20). However, Christians have chosen to take this pagan holiday and reload it with a Christian meaning. If Christians do not choose to celebrate the pagan fertility symbols of Easter bunnies and eggs, I totally agree. It is unfortunate that Easter has become such a commercialized holiday. Yet I do prefer that people remember Christ instead of the goddess Astarte each Easter!

The challenge we face is to effectively engage a culture that is steeped in non-Biblical traditions. Religious traditions are like bricks forming a wall that separates people from God. People aren't crossing over to God because they can't see beyond the wall. We should take some of those bricks down and use them to build a bridge to God instead.

One of the typical phrases Thai Buddhists are familiar with is *"gerd, gai, jep, tai"* which is a very concise way of saying "everybody who is born suffers from old age, illness and death". That is the Buddhist view of life. I like to take this familiar phrase and infuse it with Christian faith and humor, *"gerd, gai, suk, sabai"* which is describing the alternative for believers, "we are born and get older, happier, healthier and wealthier!" Buddhists always crack a smile when I say this, because it's infusing Christ into a sad world.

Rather than ignore or worse argue against Buddhist sayings, I put some life and joy into them! Getting old with Christ is not a sad thing. Every day of Christian life is a day closer to Heaven!

Christianity that tries to share God's love while turning a blind eye to Buddhism has not worked. Buddhism engages the culture it enters and adapts. It blends with Taoism in China, mixes with Shinto in Japan, and extols individual freedom in the West. Christianity needs to engage Buddhism soon and adapt our *methods* without compromising our *message*. One way we can do this is by finding a common starting point, the words of Buddha, and building a bridge to the words of Christ.

If you are more comfortable preaching the Gospel without referring to Buddhism, I am for you and what you are doing! You can still reach a few converts, but you will probably experience many difficulties with discipleship. Buddhism is all they know. They will not learn Christianity until they unlearn some long-held Buddhist assumptions. As Alan Johnson discovered during his mission work in Thailand, "In my experience a large part of the sharing of our faith is first the correcting of misunderstanding before one can move to the heart of the message."[3] Unless you directly address core Buddhist beliefs, using Buddhist vocabulary and redeeming what is good, you will keep seeing uncommitted converts who are easily influenced by their old traditions. The best thing a person who won't address Buddhist teachings can do is to preach the Gospel instead of anti-Buddhism. If you will not build bridges to Buddhists, at least try not to burn them!

# 32

# IS BUDDHA IN HEAVEN?

We have discovered that Buddha had a lot of insight. Buddha taught the four great truths which parallel what the Bible teaches. The first two truths are the themes of the Old Testament; the final two truths are the subjects of the New Testament.

We have discovered that Buddha taught the parable of the four lotus, which sounds a lot like Jesus' parable of the four soils. Buddha compared humanity to four different levels of lotus. Jesus compared the human heart to four different types of soils. Both of them were saying that not everyone we preach to is going to bear fruit; only about one quarter of the people who read or hear instruction will actually be paying attention and applying the lessons to their lives.

It's very interesting how much Jesus and Buddha had in common. Christians can't deny the fact that Buddha discovered some truths. However, Christians shouldn't blindly accept everything Buddhism or any other religion says.

I believe that people who sincerely search for truth will come across some light. For the Bible says that if you search for God you will find Him.

**JEREMIAH 29:13**

**13 And you will seek Me and find Me, when you search for Me with all your heart.**

This question used to bother me, "What happens to people who live in the Amazon or some remote part of the earth who never had the chance to hear the Good News of Jesus Christ?" It's no longer a big puzzle to me. If anyone truly *wants* to know the truth, God will spare no resource to send them a messenger (a person, a book, a CD, a video) which will proclaim Christ to them. I am convinced that God is fair to everyone who searches for Him with all their heart.

God has answered my question not only through His Word, but by taking me to the Amazon! I think God has a sense of humor. I can report that while many Western intellectuals think the "primitive people" are ignorant of the Bible, many of them have in fact already been evangelized. Meanwhile those who live in big modern cities often have the easiest access to good Biblical teaching, but are completely ignorant of the New Testament truths.

Not knowing God is not a problem of geography, but an issue of the human heart. No matter where we are or what time period we live in, God is able to reach our hearts if we truly *want* Him. Do you really think He could resist a repentant heart when He sees it?

**PSALM 34:18**

**18 The LORD is near to those who have a broken heart, and saves such as have a contrite spirit.**

I cannot draw a conclusion about Buddha's eternal status because I don't know him personally. None of us know Buddha's heart. All we know are stories that have been passed down for over two thousand years. He could have been a man who truly searched for the living God. And if he had searched with all his heart, there's a promise in the Bible written since 600BC, "Seek Me, and you will find Me." I think this applies to Buddha as well as to any of us. There is

evidence, particularly from his last words, that Buddha may
have had a relationship with God.

# 33

# THE LAST WORDS OF JESUS

**M**ARK 16:15-16
15 Go into ALL THE WORLD and preach the Gospel to every creature.

16 He who believes and is baptized will be saved; but he who does not believe will be condemned.

**MATTHEW 28:19**

Go therefore and make disciples of ALL NATIONS.

These are the last words of Jesus. This is called the Great Commission, or the last command Jesus gave to His believers. Just before Jesus ascended back up to Heaven, He gave Christians a mandate to go and reach every nation. Does that include Buddhist nations? Absolutely! Does that include Hindu and Muslim nations? Absolutely! It includes all nations.[1]

## OFFENSIVE & INTOLERANT?

There are two secular arguments creeping into society against the Great Commission. The first is that the idea of converting someone from one religion to another is offensive. The second is that evangelism is intolerant.

L et's take the second argument first. If tolerance were the goal, then secularists need to be tolerant of the fact that Christians believe Christ, and Christ commissioned His true disciples to go into all the world and preach the Gospel to every person. To disrespect that Christian belief would be a flagrant violation of tolerance!

I have found that the most intolerant people in the world tend to silence their opponents. The only way I know to cultivate tolerance is to communicate freely and exchange ideas without fear. We need to create bridges of understanding so we can communicate and share what we believe with each other more effectively.

T he first argument against the Great Commission of Jesus Christ is that it is offensive to convert people. Says who? It is a human right, guaranteed by God and spelled out in the *Universal Declaration of Human Rights* by the United Nations, that anyone can change their religion. Did you know that? It is a human right and no one has the moral authority to take away freedom of speech, freedom of conscience, and freedom to change religion. To silence people's conscience and voice is the most offensive violation of human rights!

Ultimately none of us can convert anyone. It takes God's power to transform a heart and change a life. But we all have the right to be informed about various systems of beliefs so that we can decide what is *true*. Ravi Zacharias aptly said that we should not sacrifice truth at the altar of respect. Buddha respected the Brahman priests, but he believed they were wrong. God will respect a person's choice to believe in things even though they are untrue. However, "respect for the right of another to be wrong does not mean that the wrong is right."[2]

When Christians obey the Great Commission, some intolerant people may persecute us, some may want to harm us, and in some countries they may even try to kill us. But we must keep pressing on because Jesus has commanded all Christians to go share the Good News at any cost, because He has paid the ultimate price for man's freedom from sin.

So many people in the world grew up without knowing who Jesus really is or why Jesus came. Millions in that category were born into Buddhist families and never had a parent who taught them to search for God or investigate the claims of the Bible. How, then, are *you* being a Christian witness to them?

## WHAT ARE WE WAITING FOR?

We all know that Jesus desires every Christian to be a witness for Him. Is this something that we are proactively obeying? Day by day and in our prayers, are we saying, "God, who is ready to hear the Good News? Lord, show me who's next! Give me the opportunity to tell someone!"? We can become so busy that we forget God's number one priority. We can lose focus on the fact that God has five billion other people who don't know Him yet. 150,000 of them die and slip away into eternity every day. He paid for their souls as much as He paid for ours.

So what are we waiting for?

Let's take a look at the various reasons why some Christians do not take the Great Commission seriously or have never led anyone to the Lord.

Firstly, some people just don't know how to. That's the honest truth. So many churches are so "seeker-friendly" that they do not teach their members how to evangelize. I know that's true, and you probably know that's true. How many sermons a year do you hear about, "Here's how you witness to a Buddhist. Here's how to witness to an atheist. Here's how to overcome the objections of an evolutionary thinker"? Is it any wonder that Christian children tend to be more easily persuaded by their worldly friends than by the church?

We've got to deal with these issues if we ever expect the church to have the confidence to get up and go, and have the boldness to share their faith to the world! This is why I'm making a concerted effort to help you to understand Buddhists, so when you meet the next Buddhist, you won't have the typical conversation: "Hi, I'm Christian. Did you know God loves you so much He died on the Cross for you?" which will nearly always be met by, "Well, I am Buddhist."

What a conversation stopper! Many Christians will give up with that reply. That's all it takes for many Christians to give up fighting for the eternal soul of someone else. They give us a one liner, "I'm a Buddhist," now what do you say?

I say, "Wow, really you're a Buddhist? I'm really interested in Buddhism. In fact, I'm reading a book on Buddhism! That's awesome to hear. So how are you doing? Are you able to keep the 5 golden rules of Buddha?" The conversation is now open and lively again!

Most of the time, the Buddhist will feel a responsibility to himself and to you to remember the five golden rules of Buddha.

"What are they again?" he thinks to himself. If he is really put on the spot, I help him out, "Do you know the five rules of Buddha? You know the first one, right? You can't kill."

"O, yes," he will usually reply, "I don't kill, I never kill."

"But do you eat meat?"

"O, yes, I do that all the time!"

"So you break the first rule of Buddha." I will go on to ask about the other rules, "Have you ever stolen anything?"

"Yes, but only small things."

"How much do you have to steal before you become a thief? The value of what you steal doesn't matter. God is looking at the heart. So you don't keep the second rule of Buddhism either... How about the third prohibition? Have you ever lied?"

"Yes, but just white lies."

"But a lie is a lie, right? Would Buddha tell a white lie? The Bible warns us that all liars will have their part in the Lake of Fire."

You can go through the rest of the rules of Buddha and he will come to the realization that he would be a better Buddhist by getting saved! He would have more chance of keeping the five rules of Buddha by being born again!

We're not adversarial and we're not fighting them. We are their friends and we are using the law of God, which Buddha just reiterated, to awaken their conscience. Moses had already outlined these laws long before Buddha ever spoke them. But we're using the law of God in a way that is familiar to them. Then we take them from what is familiar to what is unfamiliar. Now that's what evangelism is all about.

The best help we can get is from the Holy Spirit. We need to learn to be sensitive to the Holy Spirit. Learn to ask Him in your heart, "What is this person familiar with? What would they understand? What are they interested in?" You'll be surprised how many times something will seem to leap into your spirit. It may be sports, it may be finance, it may be another religion, it might be something else entirely. Just go ahead and use that as a conversation primer, because there is some truth to be picked in every field of knowledge. It's the beauty of life, really.

If you are wise in any area of life, you know that you need to ask help. The richest people have learned to take advice and seek education from other professionals. Top athletes still need to listen to coaches and dieticians. The best singers in the world need vocal trainers and managers. Even great authors need an editor! None of us can be objective about ourselves. Whenever we want to succeed, we need to seek expert help. If our problem is sin, we need to look for Someone Sinless to give us direction.

I t's so simple to connect what people are familiar with to the message of the Bible, because everything created by God points to His Son Jesus Christ, specifically to His death, burial and resurrection. Jesus once told His disciples, "Have you ever noticed how a seed sown dies and afterwards it brings forth much life? Have you ever considered how that agricultural cycle is pointing to Me?" (John 12:24 paraphrased). God sowed His Son into the earth, His Son died, and afterwards His Resurrection brought forth much life. Every day the sun sets, disappears, then rises again. Every day, you lay your body to rest, tuck yourself under the cover, and if you are fortunate, you will rise again the next day! Everything in life is a reminder of Jesus' death, burial and resurrection. Everything is about Him because He is the Creator of every good thing.

The first thing we must overcome to obey Jesus' Great Commission is the lack of knowledge that destroys people (Hosea 4:6). Christians do nothing because we don't know what to say. Christians usually don't know what to say to Buddhists. By the time you finish this book, you will have eliminated that problem. You will know too much to say! Many Buddhists I encounter do not know a fraction of what you have already learned. So you only need to say a fraction of what you've learned and you would get more people saved.

The second thing we must overcome to obey Jesus' Great Commission is the fear of man. I don't know about other countries, but this fear grips Australians like a plague. We may not bow down to idols, we may not suffer much poverty, but we've got our own problems, and I think this one tops them all: the paralyzing fear of man.

I have known and prayed for pastors who are gripped with the fear of man. One pastor in Australia told me that he is afraid to go to his own church! He is afraid of the people there. Jesus says to us, "Fear not![3] Greater is He who is in you than he who is in the world (1 John 4:4)!" If God is with us, shouldn't we behave like overcomers? We must speak to the fear and say boldly, "I will not fear!" Fear is the devil's way of cheating us of our destiny and tricking us into living below God's best for us.

**JOHN 14:12**

**12 Most assuredly, I say to you, he who believes in Me, the works that I do he will do also; and greater works than these he will do, because I go to My Father.**

Jesus said you can do the works that He did and you can do greater works than those! Jesus healed lepers, raised the dead, unstopped deaf ears, opened blind eyes and He said that you can do the same. Never mind the "greater" part yet, let's just do the same works that He did! You as a believer have the power in Jesus' Name!

The devil knows this is true about you. His only hope is that you don't ever come to realize who you really are and what you really can do in Christ. If you do come to realize it, his last resort is to try to make you too afraid to ever prove God's Word out.

Tell someone the Good News, lay hands on the sick, and watch the Holy Spirit work to confirm His own Word. God's Word works! I have been to many countries and prayed for many sick people, regardless of their religions, and seen God perform many healings. Some have been gradual, others instant, but any degree of healing is better than staying sick, wouldn't you agree? Thanks be to God!

God told Jeremiah, "Do not be afraid of their faces, for I

am with you to deliver you, says the LORD" (1:8). Don't be afraid of people's faces, robes, idols, amulets, or anything strange and foreign. God is with you. Go out and spread the Good News! What's going to happen when somebody sick gets healed? They're just going to be grateful they met you! What if some reject your message? I've lived long enough to know this: "no" doesn't mean "never." Right now may not be the time when they are most open. Commit them in prayer and go on to the next person who is searching for truth or help.

There are at least five billion people who haven't heard the Gospel. There are lots of takers, lots of people who will say "yes" to God's free gift of salvation! We're just out delivering God's Gift to those who have a readiness and willingness to receive. Don't wait. Don't hold back. Overcome your fears by faith. Put God first and the anointing of the Holy Spirit will be with you as you shine your light!

# WHAT WOULD BUDDHA SAY?

If Buddha could speak today, what would he say?

I believe Buddha would continue to tell people to look for a way to avoid Hell at any cost. He was willing to leave his caste, leave his wealth, leave his religion, leave his ancestor's man-made traditions, and suffer any price to be set free from karma.[1]

How many Buddhists are willing to leave all to find salvation? Jesus said this is what is required. In Matthew 5:29-30, Jesus told the world to avoid Hell at any cost: "If your right eye causes you to sin, pluck it out and cast it from you; for it is more profitable for you that one of your members perish, than for your whole body to be cast into Hell. And if your right hand causes you to sin, cut it off and cast it from you; for it is more profitable for you that one of your members perish, than for your whole body to be cast into Hell." Jesus and Buddha agreed that any price, any persecution, is worth missing the eternal flames of Hell. Jesus and Buddha had much in common!

If Buddha had the chance, he would have rejoiced to converse with a Christian and ponder with gratitude the thought that his Creator has suffered the punishment of all sins for humanity. Perhaps Buddha saw this, or else how could he have prophesied so precisely about the Coming Savior? God does not dwell in the realm of time. God saw Jesus Christ as "the Lamb slain from the foundation of the world" (Revelation 13:8). Could God not have shown this to Buddha before it happened in time?

If Buddha were alive today, I have no doubt in my mind that he would be in church and reading the Bible. If Buddha were alive today, he would say to Buddhists, "Reform your religion. Stop bowing down to idols. I left Hinduism because I detested its myriad of idols. Stop playing with superstitions.[2] I taught you to reason. Have a conversation with a Christian. Meditate deeply on the price that the only sinless King paid for the redemption of all slaves. Be thankful to Christ. He did what no one else could have done." These would be the last words of Buddha.

APPENDIX

**How reliable are the records of Buddhist prophecies and stories?**

No one can prove what Buddha originally taught. Unlike Christians, Buddhists simply do not have original manuscripts that date to the time of Buddha. Nor can anyone prove that the current Buddhist teachings have not been corrupted after 2500 years. All we can do is piece together the evidence forensically to the best of our ability.

I am grateful for the efforts of one former monk *Tongsuk Siriruk* who in 1954 recorded some of Buddhist stories that are useful for Christians. Others have questioned his credibility.

While I have no interest to defend him, my interest is only to defend the Gospel, some comments from me may be appropriate since the deceased man cannot answer for himself. Tongsuk left the Buddhist monkhood and became a Christian. Anyone who leaves his traditions will have critics. (Buddha had his critics when he abandoned Hinduism.) But despite the criticism, I think his material is worth looking at.

First, Tongsuk received permission from *Pra-Siwisuttiwong* (deputy abbot in Bangkok) to copy the *Tripitaka* in *Wat-*

*Prasing*[1] in Chiangmai. His copy was certified as accurate by his village head on 13 October 1954.

Second, Chiangmai is the historical location of the authorized Pali text in Thailand, which was revised at the Thai 8th Buddhist Council in 1477. Where better to copy the original Buddhist texts?

Third, Tongsuk referred to Buddhist texts with antiquated terms such as *Praputta-jarot Pook 5*. *Praputta-jarot* means "words of Buddha". *Pook* here refers to palm leafs (*bai lan*) tied together (*pook*) by one string (*sai sanong*). This was the old way of keeping Buddhist texts. Modern monks no longer refer to *pook* but to books (*lem*).

Fourth, Tongsuk referred to the *Kampee Khom* or Cambodian (Khmer) Sacred Text. The Mon-Khmer people were the dominant people group living in the area extending from present day Myanmar to Cambodia; they were the first Theravada Buddhists in Southeast Asia. When the Tai people, which includes people from Hainan (south-eastern island of China) to Assam (north-eastern state of India), immigrated to present day Thailand, they brought with them beliefs in Mahayana Buddhism. Thais converted to Theravada[2] after coming into contact with the Mon-Khmers. The Thai alphabet came from the Khmer alphabet[3]. Thai Buddhism came from Khmer Buddhism. Therefore it seems likely that we would find the earliest, unabridged stories of Buddha from the Khmer Text.

Fifth, every teaching Tongsuk referred to is standard Buddhist doctrine. What may be found in today's *Tripitaka*, he communicated faithfully and accurately. There is no reason to doubt him when he recorded what may no longer be found in later versions of the *Tripitaka*.

Sixth, Tongsuk was a genuine Buddhist monk who became a genuine follower of Jesus Christ. No believer wants to lie, for in both Buddhism and Christianity, "all liars will have their part in the lake of fire."

Seventh, there were 2261 years between the Third Council (where the Theravada text was agreed upon) and the Last Council in Burma (where modern revisions were made). If doubt was to be cast on anything, it should be cast on the latest revision. Since Christianity was well known by the 20th century, some stories that sounded too Christian may have been removed from the Buddhist texts. I do not say that this was done deliberately or maliciously, but may had been done subconsciously or sincerely to prevent confusion.

Eighth, the critics tend to be young and do not remember that many Thai elders talked of Buddha's predictions of the One coming after him who will have scars in His hands, feet, and side. This is common knowledge among the older generation. I have talked to many Buddhists who are familiar with this prophecy. It is impossible that they were all "evangelized" during the early 20th century, since we are now well into the 21st century and still less than 1% of Thailand is evangelical Christian. It is more likely they were getting their information from early Buddhist texts.

Ninth, if we go back to the root of Buddhism, which was Hinduism, we can find similar predictions of the coming Savior of the world. This is common knowledge among Hindus who study the Vedas. I have asked several of my Indian friends if they have heard of Buddha's own prediction of the coming Savior with pierced hands, feet and side, and they have told me it is common knowledge. If that knowledge has survived in India for 2500 years, and non-Buddhists can still recall it, should not the older Buddhists still recall this story?

# NOTES

## PREFACE ABOUT LANGUAGE

1. The Latin Bible is called the *Vulgate* and was the official Bible of the Catholic Church until 1979.
2. The Protestant Reformation officially started in 1517 when Martin Luther *protested* the Catholic ideas that the Pope was infallible, the church could sell salvation (called 'indulgences'), and no one but the clergy could understand the Bible. Protestants emphasize that the Bible is the only infallible source of truth, salvation is by faith in Christ alone, and everyone in the world who *wants* to understand the Bible can. Interestingly, one of the most common questions Buddhists ask is, "What's the difference between Catholic and Protestant?"
3. The Bible continues to be the most translated book in the world. The Bible exists in over 2300 languages out of the 6000+ known languages, and can now be accessed in many hotels, over the Internet and even by cellular phones! http://www.biblesociety.org/latestnews/latest232-slr2002stats.html
4. Pope John XXIII and the Second Vatican Council decided to permit the use of the vernacular in masses (or Catholic services). Prior to that, the commoner did not understand what was said in service.
5. Asians refer to Pali-Sanskrit the way Westerners refer to Greco-Roman. Although they are two different and separate influences, yet throughout history, they have become inextricably intertwined.

## INTRODUCTION

1. Hawaii contains a large population of Chinese, Japanese and Korean immigrants, most of whom are some type of Buddhist.

## 2. THE STORY OF THE EEL

1. Thai: *pla lai*.
2. Some Westerners may be quite happy to never eat eel, but many Asians love it. The Japanese grill it with Teriyaki sauce and it is quite nice.
3. Thai: *Platoo Nam*.
4. Thai for "to pay back for the release of sin." *Sadau* literally means hit, beat, or chase out. *Kro* is short for *kro gum wain gum*, literally "unexpected evil of karma; revenge of karma," or simply "evil karma

retributive karma." *Sadau kro* requires performance of a good deed that usually involves buying something; e.g. buying birds or eels and releasing them. This probably descended from the Old Testament practice of releasing the scapegoat into the wilderness (Leviticus 16:22) and releasing a clean bird dipped in blood into the open field (Leviticus 14:6). The Old Testament practice predated Buddha by 3000 years, and was codified by the time of Moses 1000 years before Buddha. Southeast Asia, of course, doesn't have native goats, so they could have substituted the Biblical practice with other things like pigs, chicken, eels or even flowers. If you don't want to perform the deed, you can pay a monk to do it for you.

5. Thai: *buad* or become a nun.
6. In Buddhist countries, many taxi drivers place idols on their car dashboard in hope of protection. I have often wondered how effective this superstition could be since in any head on collision, the idols would nearly always be first to break through the windshield!

## 3. EAST MEETS WEST

1. Matthew 2:2, 8:2, 14:33, 28:9, 17; John 13:12, 20:28-29
2. John 3:15-16, 36; 5:24, 6:47.
3. Thai: *nippan.*
4. Thai: *duang.*
5. Thai: *suoy.*
6. Einstein's *General Theory of Relativity* proves that time and matter are connected, therefore if matter had a beginning, then time also had a beginning. Since everything that has a beginning has a cause, the beginning of time and matter demand a First Cause.

   The *Second Law of Thermodynamics* or *Entropy* states that the universe is declining from a state of order to disorder, therefore an infinitely old universe would be infinitely disorderly (with no life or usable energy left). Since there are order, biological information and usable energy, the universe cannot be infinitely old, but must have had a beginning. Someone in the beginning ordered it.

## 4. THE THIN BUDDHA, FAT BUDDHA & LAUGHING BUDDHA

1. You can read about the different sects of Buddhism in the chapter *Which Denomination?*
2. Thai: *Pra-see-ariya-med-trai-yo,* which Thais like to shorten to either *Pra-see-arn* or *Pra-med-trai.*
3. According to the Bible Peter was married (Mark 1:30) and the other apostles were married (1 Cor 9:5). Although Paul wasn't married, he

recommended to both Titus and Timothy to find bishops who were (1 Tim 3:1-2, Titus 1:6-7) and commended marriage as honourable (Heb 13:4). There is no Biblical command to not marry, and one that specifically says to *not* forbid marriage (1 Tim 4:2-3).

## 5. WHO WAS BUDDHA?

1. This is probably a corruption of the true Messianic prophecy. Even the name *Maitriya* is reminiscent of the *Messiah*. The Jews, Muslims, and some Buddhists, rightly believe that there is a Perfect, Sinless One who will be coming back. His name is Jesus.
2. There is a *Lumpini Park* in Bangkok named after Buddha's birthplace.
3. *Brahmins* are nobles of the highest caste of Indian society. (Not to be confused with *brahmans* – the priests of Hindu religion.) These 8 *brahmins* were evidently prophets.
4. Sanskrit: *Guandinya*. Pali: *Kondanna*.
5. Unlike many Western countries which have 4 seasons, that part of the world has only 3 seasons: hot, cold and rainy.
6. His mother's niece.
7. Sanskrit: *avidya*. Pali: *avijja*. English: delusion, ignorance. Related to *maya*, which for Hindus is the illusion or fleeting reality of life and the universe. In both Buddhism and Christianity, there can be no salvation unless one sees there is more to life than what we see. God and Heaven are real.
8. The goal of being liberated from suffering is called *moksha* or *mukti*.
9. For a full survey of world religions and cults on DVD, please visit www.discover.org.au/catalog.
10. *Sujata* actually thought he was a ghost because he was so emaciated.
11. This type of fig tree is large like a banyan tree and is known locally as the *Bodhi tree*.
12. December 8 is celebrated as the day Siddhartha Gautama sat under the *Bodhi tree*.
13. Sanskrit: *arhat*. Pali: *arahant*. English: one who has escaped *samsara* (reincarnation) and achieved *nirvana* (extinction).
14. Pali-Sanskrit: *arya-sangha*. English: noble company of monks.

## 6. THE LOTUS PARABLE

1. 1 Corinthians 15:6, Luke 24:49, Acts 1:4-8
2. Acts 1:15
3. In a similar way,
4. Proverbs 8:17, Jeremiah 29:13, Matthew 7:7-8
5. By comparison, Jesus ministered for 3 ½ years and produced more leaders and believers than anyone before Him or since. When his first

disciple Peter preached for the first time, 3000 became Christian (Acts 2:41). After his second sermon, 5000 became Christian (Acts 4:4).

6. Pali-Sanskrit word meaning 'bliss'. Sometimes Ananda did substitute-teaching for Buddha. He is known in some Buddhist tradition as the second patriarch of Buddhism. From India to Thailand, *Ananda* has become a common boy's name because he was Buddha's favorite disciple.

7. February 15 is Nirvana Day, commemorating Buddha's death. His passing was not marked by any particular miracle or sign of enlightenment, but by food poisoning. The Christian parallel is Easter or the Day of Resurrection, commemorating Jesus' triumph over man's greatest enemy. Jesus defeated death.

8. Prior to Westernization, Buddhists did not use what we call the "Year of the Lord" or *Anno Domini* (A.D.) in Latin. Instead, Buddhists use the approximate date of Buddha's enlightenment as a starting point. If you would like to know what year it is on the Buddhist calendar, simply add 543 to the current year. For instance, the Christian year 2000 A.D. would be 2543 in some Buddhist countries.

## 8. THE FOUR NOBLE TRUTHS

1. Pali: *ariyasaccani*. Sanskrit: *aryasatyani*. Thai: *ariya sat si*, literally "noble truths four".

2. I will give the Thai pronunciation first, then the Pali-Sanskrit second.

3. Indians call it *karma*. Thais call it *gum* or *wain gum* or to be most precise *kro gum wain gum*.

4. Any parent knows that the free will of a child is very powerful. No matter how much you love your child and teach him right, if he chooses to trust in drug pushers or criminals, their mistrust of you and their trust in wrong friends could lead to death. On the other hand, their trust in your wisdom, even when they don't understand it yet, could save their lives. God like a good Father wants us to trust Him because our faith in Him will save us.

5. Dictionary of the Royal Institute, Aksorn Chareon Taat Publisher, Bangkok, Edition 2525 (1982), authorized by the Thai Government and approved by the Army General & Prime Minister *Prame Tinasulanon*, p. 12.

6. *Baab* is the Thai word for sin. Christians have traditionally preferred to use *baab* over the word *gum*, even though the second definition of *gum* tells us they are synonymous, and *gum* is more easily understood by Buddhists.

7. Both Buddhism and Christianity teach we are sinners from the day we are born. Buddhism teaches that if we were perfect, we would not be born at all. We would cease from being reincarnated. The Bible says we inherited our nature or our spiritual DNA from our sinful parents –

Adam & Eve. However, babies and children who die young never go to Hell because they are under the age of accountability. God does not hold them accountable until they know good from evil and choose evil voluntarily.

8. Thai: *got hang gum.*
9. Sanskrit: *moksha* or *mukti.*
10. Literally cessation of existence, but many Buddhists also believe in Heaven and Hell. The Bible teaches clearly that there is a Heaven and Hell.

## 9. THE POLIO VICTIM

1. Thai: *Samret arahan* or reach the highest level of life.
2. Thai: *buad hai maa.*
3. Thai: *gor pa lerng kern sawan.*
4. Thai: *nang wipadsana.*
5. Thai: *suoy.*
6. Thai: *bpadt bpow* or literally "sweep blow".
7. Thai: *mai kraup 32 suan.*
8. Brahmanism teaches that the highest state of a human being is to be born a Brahmin or member of India's priestly caste. Only Brahmins have the privilege of teaching the Hindu sacred literature. Some use Brahmanism synonymously with Hinduism, while others believe it is one denomination within a larger religion. The nuance is up to the reader to decide, but the two share obvious similarities.

## 10. HOW JESUS MADE HIMSELF KNOWN

1. Thai: *lut pon jag gum* = to be set free from the power of sin.

## 11. THE FIVE COMMANDMENTS OF BUDDHA

1. The Sanskrit equivalent is *panca sila.*
2. *Benja seen* and *seen ha* are synonymous, but the latter is more commonly used nowadays.
3. Dictionary of Buddhism (Thai-English), P.A. Payutto, University of Maha Chulalongkorn Ratchawitayarai, 2546 (2003), p. 175.
4. *Ibid.* p. 175.
5. *Ibid.* p. 175.

## 13. THE KOREAN BUDDHIST

1. Despite popular misunderstanding, Christianity is *not* a Western religion. Christianity originated in the East and today some of the largest churches in the world are in Asian countries like South Korea, Singapore and Indonesia. Some of most Christian regions in the world are in Asia, South Korea is 1/3 born again, Nagaland in northeastern India claims to be 80% born again. There are millions of Christians in the persecuted churches of China!
2. *Bulgogi* is a delicious barbeque meat. Try it next time you're at a Korean restaurant!
3. For more audio or video teachings on *Financial Breakthrough*, *Secrets of the Rich* or *business* as a call, please visit www.discover.org.au/catalog.

## 14. THE TEN KARMAS

1. Thai: *gumma bot sip (10)*.
2. Thai: *hon-taang hang gum sip (10) yaang serng ja tum hai mannut pai soo narok*.

## 15. IS THERE A HELL?

1. Thai: *maan*; Pali: *mara*.
2. Thai: *dok pai nai grata-tongdang*
3. Thai: *peen ton ngew*. The scientific name for this tree *ton ngew* is the *Bombax ceiba*, a tropical tree whose trunk bears spikes and thorns.
4. Sacred text of Buddhism. You can learn more about it in the chapter *The Three Baskets*.
5. Thai: *kum*.
6. Thai: *Baa na, ter ja tok Narok Away-jee!*
7. *Kampan Sudcha* of the *Lower Isaan Foundation for Enablement (LIFE)* uses this style of witnessing.
8. Matthew 25:41
9. Luke 16:24 – I owe it to Jesus and Bill Wiese for helping me see how terrible Hell really is!
10. Revelation 14:10
11. Psalm 88:6
12. Psalm 127:2, Revelation 14:11
13. Psalm 88:8
14. Hosea 13:8
15. Psalm 106:41, Deuteronomy 28:29
16. Revelation 13:6, John 15:18

## 16. REINCARNATION

1. According to Barna Research, Oct 21, 2003. www.barna.org/FlexPage.aspx?Page=BarnaUpdate&BarnaUpdateID=150
2. That is, go to Nirvana. Nirvana strictly means going out of existence, but if you say going to Heaven, many Buddhists would accept that.
3. Thai: *kro gum wain gum*
4. Thai: *nippan*. Literally, cessation of existence.
5. Scott Noble, *The Buddhist Road Map*, http://www.letusreason.org/Buddh7.htm, referring to Ernest Valea, *Past-life recall as modern proof for reincarnation*, www.comparativereligion.com/reincarnation1.html
6. Thai: *wain wai dai gerd*.

## 17. WOMEN IN BUDDHISM

1. The "One Child Policy" instituted by Deng Xiaoping in 1979 should properly be called the "One Birth Policy" because Chinese mothers are allowed to give birth to twins.
2. Thailand has *mae chee's* or non-ordained women who have vowed celibacy and renounced worldly living.
3. The Australian (March 20 2008) *Resigning crosses church-state line.*

## 18. KING ASOKA & THE PYTHON

1. Thai: *seen*. Remember the minimum commandments for a Buddhist to keep are the 5 prohibitions or *seen ha*. This man kept more than the five! This is what this story is referring to – keeping all the *seen*.
2. Thai: *pla siew*.
3. Thai: *pla-jom* – a nice Asian dish.
4. Thai: *tum*. Pali: *tamma*. Sanskrit: *dharma*.
5. Thai: *boon*.
6. Thai: *pit seen pana*.

## 19. JESUS ON REINCARNATION

1. Do good deeds that count as "merit", such as feeding monks in the morning. Make merit.

## 20. THE KING & THE UNGRATEFUL DEBTOR

1. Working seven days a week, of course, is a sin. It breaks God's fourth commandment of keeping at least 1 day a week for God. It is a case of a sinner trying to sin his way out of sin. While he is working to pay off his sin, he adds more sins.
2. The Hebrews start their day in rest, which is a type of Christ. It is out of rest or Christ that we have strength for each day. In Genesis chapter 1, God calls each "evening and morning," *not* "morning to evening," a full day. God never ends the day in darkness. With God, things always move from darkness to light, and our days always get brighter!
3. Bloomberg.com, Kristin Hensen & Timothy Burger, *Clinton Earns $10.7 Million*, 14 June 2007.
4. Romans 8:17, Galatians 4:7
5. Romans 8:37
6. Ephesians 1:20
7. Wealth is more than money. It is time, peace of mind, protection from God, opportunities that money cannot buy. To grow in the knowledge of who you are and what you have in Christ, and your true authority because of Christ, I have compiled some empowering Scriptures in my booklet *Zoe Life Reality* available from www.discover.org.au/catalog.

## 22. THE LAST WORDS OF BUDDHA

1. Thai: *gilead* or innate corruption.
2. Full title: *Pra-see-ariya-med-trai-yo*, which Thais tend to shorten to either *Pra-see-arn* or *Pra-medtrai*.
3. Thai: *prahm*, one of the Hindu priests.
4. Thai: *asongkai*. This is an ancient word for an indefinitely long time. In context, the meaning of the word is unclear.
5. Thai: *gongjak* – a sharp cutting wheel with jagged edges, an ancient weapon.
6. Thai for *nirvana*.

## 23. WHICH DENOMINATION?

1. Thai: *nikai*, Pali: *nikaya*.
2. Catholics and Protestants divided in 1517 over the issue of the Biblical authority and the Pope's power. Protestants believe in the supremacy of the Bible over all human institution. A similar divide occurred in 1054 between Roman Catholics and Eastern Orthodox, over a similar issue of the Roman Pope's power.

3. There is a third and more nationalistic sect of Buddhism, called Tibetan Buddhism or Vajrayana, literally the Diamond Vehicle.

4. A brief biography of King Asoka may be found the chapter *King Asoka & the Python*.

5. Thai: *Hinayan*. *Hina* is Sanskrit for "little" and *yana* for "vehicle". *Hinayana* means Little Vehicle or path to enlightenment.

6. Thai: *Terawad*.

7. Thai: *Mahayan*. *Maha* is Sanskrit for "big" and *yana* for "vehicle". *Mahayana* means the Big Vehicle or path to enlightenment.

8. Zen Buddhism was founded by *Bodhi-dharma*, an Indian monk in China who arrived in Japan in 538AD.

9. Chinese: *Guan Yin*. Thai: *Guan Im*.

10. *Vajra* is Sanskrit for "diamond" and *yana* for "vehicle".

11. Called the Mahayana Sutras.

12. A bodhisattva is a saintlike person who has postponed nirvana to help other attain enlightenment. In practice, they are worshipped and prayed to like gods and goddesses who can grant wishes and protection.

13. The most famous being the *Bardo Thodol* or the Tibetan Book of the Dead.

14. *Dalai* is Mongolian for "Ocean" and *Lama* is Tibetan for "Guru or Monk".

15. Matthew Philips, *China Regulates Buddhist Reincarnation*, Newsweek Aug 20-27, 2007. Available at: www.tibet.ca/en/wtnarchive/2007/8/23_5.html

## 24. THE THREE BASKETS (TRIPITAKA)

1. All versions of the Bible in every language contain the same stories. (Some Catholic Bibles add a few extra books in the *Apocrypha*, but do not change the content of the universally accepted books.) The preservation of the Bible is a veritable miracle. Some people worry that the Bible may have been corrupted. However by 300BC, the Old Testament had been translated from Hebrew into Latin; and by 150AD, the New Testament had been translated from Greek into Latin, Syriac, Coptic, and many foreign languages. Since the Bible is the most translated and most quoted book in the world, for anyone to "doctor" it, they would not only have to change their own copy of the Bible, but thousands of others in many foreign languages and thousands of quotes made by scholars like Irenaeus, Origen, Tertullian... a feat that, if it were possible, would be a bigger miracle than God's ability to preserve the Bible's purity!

2. http://www.akshin.net/literature/budlitsourceschina.htm

3. http://www.akshin.net/literature/budlitsourcespali.htm

4. Exodus 17:14, 34:27, Deuteronomy 27:3

5. Deuteronomy 11:20
6. Deuteronomy 17:18
7. Isaiah 8:1, 30:8, Jeremiah 30:2, Habakkuk 2:2, Luke 1:3, Revelation 1:11
8. Thai: *bai lan*. Cambodian: *slek rit*.
9. Thai: *sai sanong*.
10. Thai for "tied together".
11. Born Thong Duang (1737-1802), he assumed the royal title of "Buddha Yodfa Chulaloke" and was posthumously titled "Rama I". He was the first king of the present Chakri Dynasty and first to appoint a *Sangha-Raja* (literally the 'Raj of the Religious Community' or Supreme Patriarch of Thai Buddhism). Rama I also moved Siam's capital from Thonburi to Bangkok and built the famous *Wat Pra Kaew* housing the Emerald Buddha, which he captured from Vientianne, Laos.

## 25. THE SIX BUDDHIST COUNCILS

1. Thai: *maha-pari-nippan*, that is, to die without coming back.
2. Maha-Gasapa was one of the first five disciples of Buddha and one of three Gasapa brothers who converted from Hinduism to Buddhism. Maha-Gasapa means the "Great Gasapa". Mahayana Buddhism claims that Maha-Gasapa reincarnated as Ji-Gong, the meat-loving, wine-bibbing Chinese monk. In Chinese Taoism, Ji-Gong is given the status of a god from Heaven and is worshipped as Daoji. Whether Maha-Gasapa reincarnated as Ji-Gong or Daoji, it would truly be a demotion from Buddhahood and a contradiction to Buddhist teaching. If anyone after Buddha achieved Buddhahood, it is assumed that at least the first five disciples of Buddha would have. If they did not, then it is unlikely that anyone since could ever hope to escape karma!
3. There are major discrepancies in dates relating to Buddhist events. I opted to pick most dates from www.wikipedia.com because I find that the exactitude of dates is irrelevant to the teachings of Buddha and Christian efforts to love Buddhists.

## 26. KING NARESUAN

1. Literally, Prince or King Naresuan (1555-1605). He is a famous hero in Thai history and recent movies made about him have added to his fame among Thais.
2. http://www.letusreason.org/Buddh7.htm

## 27. SUMMARY

1. In university level science classes, which I took, it was always drummed into us at every opportunity that the earth is millions of years old. One obvious problem with that is the math – the total human population was only 1 billion in 1804, 500 million in 1600, 200 million at the birth of Christ (1AD). Even if we allowed 0.5% growth per year (near extinction level), working backwards, we would only get to a few people around 5000 years ago (the time of Noah's Flood). If humans have existed for millions of years, where are all the prehistoric human bones? Our modern cities should be built on human bones.

   Henry Morris wrote, "It begins to be glaringly evident that the human race cannot be very old! The traditional Biblical chronology is infinitely more realistic than the million-year history of mankind assumed by the evolutionist." (www.ldolphin.org/morris.html) For more articles by scientists who challenge the conventional anti-Biblical assumptions, search keywords in www.answersingenesis.org or www.creationontheweb.org.

2. A virgin giving birth was once perceived as fanciful myth. Now we know it's possible through IVF (in-vitro-fertilization). God's technology was simply in advance of ours.

3. To authenticate His arrival on earth, God preceded it with 4000 years of prophecies, announcing ahead of time how He would come in very specific details: Genesis 3:15, Proverbs 30:4, Isaiah 7:14, Isaiah 9:6, Micah 5:2, Malachi 3:1, Matthew 1:23.

## 28. END TIME PREDICTIONS OF BUDDHA & JESUS

1. Thai: *tamnai.*
2. Sanskrit: *dharma*; Pali: *tamma.*
3. Matthew 10:21, 24:10, Luke 21:16
4. Pali-Sanskrit: *panya-dtagk-charn* or *pa-ti-sampi-tayarn.*
5. Thai: *ho hern dern agad.*
6. Thai: *wai roobp, ter phee.*
7. Pali-Sanskrit: *micha-ditthi*, or seeing wrong as right, e.g. worshipping idols, spirits, ghosts, demons.
8. If Buddha were correct, then we are less than 500 years away. However, students of the Bible expect the Return of Christ much sooner, based on observing prophecies fulfilled in Israel & the Middle East.
9. Thai: *fai-bunlai-gun.*
10. For more understanding of Biblical prophecies on End Times, visit www.discover.org.au/catalog for:
    a 3 hour CD series on the first chapters of Revelation, called

*7 Letters to 7 Churches*
a 15 hour CD series, called *End Times*.

11. Psalm 102:25-26, Isaiah 51:6, Hebrews 1:10-11
12. Spontaneous generation has never been observed. It is pure fiction.
13. Darwin did not come up with the idea of evolution, but probably borrowed it from his grandfather Erasmus Darwin, who published primitive ideas of the Big Bang and evolution in the 1790s. As for natural selection, some researchers believe Charles Darwin plagiarized it from Edward Blyth, who proposed it in the 1830s. For more information, see http://www.creationontheweb.com/content/view/387

## 29. THE AUTHORITY OF THE BIBLE

1. *Farang* is a general term for white foreigners. It originally referred to the French and came from the word "francais," which Thais pronounce *farangced*.

## 31. THE RISK OF SYNCRETISM

1. Alan Johnson, *Wrapping the Good News for the Thai*, p. 16, http://agts.edu/syllabi/ce/summer2002/mthm639oleson_sum02_np_r3.pdf
2. Roy Reinhold calculated Jesus' birthday to be exactly on September 11 3 BC, which is significant for at least two reasons: 1) That day 'happened' to be the 1st of *Tishri*, the first day of the Jewish civil (original) calendar, 2) Satan 'happened' to send his terrorists to attack the Twin Towers in New York on the same day, thereby trying to desecrate the memory of a Day of Hope into a day of terrorism. See: *Paganism in Christmas*, http://members.aol.com/prophecy04/Articles/Christianity/christmas.html, and *Exact Date of Yeshua's Birth*, http://members.aol.com/prophecy04/Articles/Yeshua/yeshuabirth1.html
3. Alan Johnson, *Wrapping the Good News for the Thai*, p.4 http://agts.edu/syllabi/ce/summer2002/mthm639oleson_-sum02_np_r3.pdf

## 33. THE LAST WORDS OF JESUS

1. To watch or listen to more of my teachings on different religions and cults, please type search at www.discover.org.au/catalog.
2. Ravi Zacharias, *The Lotus & the Cross*, Multnomah Publishers, Oregon, p. 81.
3. Matthew 10:28, Luke 8:50, Luke 12:32

## 34. WHAT WOULD BUDDHA SAY?

1. Thai: *lud pon jag baab* or to be free from sin!
2. Thai: *saiyasaad.*


# APPENDIX

1. *Wat* means "temple" in Thai. *Wat-prasing* is a common name for many temples in Chiangmai.

2. Thais actually received Theravada influence from both sides: from the Khmer in the east, and from the Burmese in the west. The Burmese conquered Lannathai in 1558 and destroyed Ayutthaya in 1767. King Taksin then relocated the Thai capital to Thonburi and drove the Burmese out of central Thailand in 1768 and out of Chiang Mai (capital of Lannathai) in 1776. Evidently letting success get to his head, Taksin declared himself a divine person (*sotapanna*), so his people rebelled and his commander executed him in 1782. In the same year, the commander moved his capital to Bang-Koh (Village Island). Although Thais call now call their capital Krung Thep, Westerners still know it by its older name Bangkok. The commander became Pra Ramathibodi or Rama I, the first king of the present Chakri dynasty.

3. When Thai monks "write blessings" (*long yan*) at the entrance of a new house or on the roof of a new taxi, or "tattoo blessings" (*long sak*) on people's bodies or boxers' arms, they still write the Pali words in *Mon-Khmer* or *Khom* script, not Thai. The most senior monks still learn both *Khom* and *Pali*. One of my Buddhist friends had a father who invited a senior abbot to *long yan* on his brand new car. Within 2 months, his second eldest son crashed his car and died at the tender age of 21. The son's best friend was a young policeman who loved his friend very much and asked for the deceased's motorcycle as a memorial. Within one month, he had a motorcycle accident and died, leaving his newly-wed wife a widow. Rather than blaming the practice of *long yan*, Thais will only seek a better monk with a bigger reputation to *long yan*. If only they knew that Jesus is the Living God who can protect them, these written blessings would have no meaning to them.

OTHER BOOKS BY STEVE
CIOCCOLANTI

**From Buddha to Jesus**
(Available in other languages including Chinese, French,
Indonesian, Japanese & Thai)
ブッダからイエスへ
(From Buddha to Jesus | Japanese Edition)
**30 Days to a New You**
(Compact Plan for Personal Growth & Freedom)
**30 Días de Renovación Personal**
(30 Days to a New You | Spanish Edition)
**12 Keys to a Good Relationship with God**
(Children's Book written with 6-year-old daughter Alexis)
**A Guide to Making a Will**
(Considering a church in your legacy)
**The Divine Code: A Prophetic Encyclopedia of Numbers,
Vol. 1 & 2** (Discover the meaning of numbers.)

All e-books are available through Amazon.com.
*The Divine Code* available as a 2-in-1 set only at
Discover.org.au

★ ★ ★ ★ ★

**Trump's Unfinished Business:
10 Prophecies to Save America**
(Make America Godly Again!)

(Paperback or Ebook)

★ ★ ★ ★ ★

VIDEOS BY STEVE CIOCCOLANTI

**7000 Years of Prophecy** (1 hour)
**End Time Complete Pack** (58 hours)
**6000 Years of History & Prophecy** (3 hours)
**4000 Years of History** (Old Testament Survey,
12 hours from Creation to Christ. Our #1 Bestseller)
**22 Future Events Predicted by Revelation** (4 hours)
**Jewish vs Christian Dating & Parenting** (2 hours)
**Where is God During Tragedies?** (2 hours)
**4 Steps to Enter into Your Call** (1 hour)
**Why Am I Not There Yet?** (1 hour)
**Atheists Don't Exists** (3 hours)
**The Life of Joseph** (6 hours)
**Defeating Fear** (3 hours)
**Book of Job** (2 hours)
**Jezebel** (2 hours)

Browse DVDs and CDs at: www.Discover.org.au
Watch videos-on-demand at:
vimeo.com/stevecioccolanti/vod_pages

# WORLD RELIGIONS LIBRARY

ISLAM
BAHAI
SIKHISM
HINDUISM
BUDDHISM
MORMONISM
HARE KRISHNAS
JEHOVAH'S WITNESSES
SEVENTH-DAY ADVENTIST
SCIENTOLOGY
GOD OF ISRAEL (Bonus DVD
when you purchase the complete library)

*WHAT PEOPLE ARE SAYING...*

*"The World Religion series equipped me to witness to people from different faiths; to go from what is familiar to them to what is familiar to us."*

*"In a pluralistic world where apparently all roads lead to the same place, the World Religions series helped me study other faiths, thus giving me boldness and confidence in sharing my own faith.:*

**Discover** Resources

Available on DVDs or CDs at:  www.DISCOVER.org.au/catalog

## Shop Online
### www.discover.org.au

## "We watched. We laughed. We got answers."

## Top Questions Series

1. Top Questions Freethinkers Ask Christians (2 DVDs)
2. Top Questions Christians Ask Pastors (1 DVD)
3. Top Questions Buddhists Ask Christians (2 DVDs)

4. Did Jesus Learn Buddhism in India?(1 DVD)
5. Top Questions Christians Ask about Hearing God (2 DVDs)
6. Top Questions about Healing (1 DVD)

## 4000 Years of History

Session 1: The Origin of the Universe: Creation or Evolution?
Session 2: The Origin of Suffering & Death
Session 3: The Origin of the Worldwide Flood Stories
Session 4: The Origin of Languages & Nations
Session 5: The Roots of Israel: Abraham, Isaac & Jacob
Session 6: Keys to Unlock the Old Testament: Moses & God's Tabernacle
Session 7: The Importance of Leadership: Joshua & Judges
Session 8: The Most Important Man in the Old Testament: David
Session 9: Wisdom to Understand the Bible: Solomon & God's Temple
Session 10: Prophets & the Prophetic
Session 11: Visions & Dreams: the Book of Daniel
Session 12: The Star of Bethlehem: Astrology or Astronomy?

## www.discover.org.au

# MEET STEVE CIOCCOLANTI

**Steve Cioccolanti**, B.A., M.Ed., is a three-time #1 Best-selling author on Amazon (see The DIVINE CODE: A Prophetic Encyclopedia of Numbers, Vol. 1 & 2). With over 42 million views, he is one of the most watched Christian YouTubers worldwide.

Watch and subscribe here:
www.YouTube.com/DiscoverMinistries
Backup channel: www.YouTube.com/DiscoverMinistriesTV

Born in Thailand to a family of Catholic, Buddhists, Methodists and Muslims, Steve Cioccolanti has a unique perspective and practical insights into spiritual life and world religions. His classic in comparative religions, From Buddha to Jesus, is one of the most influential Christian books in Thailand and Southeast Asia.

He is a prolific teacher, pastor of Discover Church, and publisher of hundreds of videos available through Vimeo.com. A sought-after speaker on personal evangelism, end-time prophecy, and Biblical justice, he has traveled to 45 countries, leads Biblical tours to the Middle East, and appears on international TV such as Daystar.

**Join his online church community via Patreon:**
www.patreon.com/cioccolanti

**To book him for your church or event, visit:**
www.discover.org.au/invite

**To join his Biblical Tours to Israel and the Middle East, visit:** www.discover.org.au/israel

Discover Ministries collects testimonies of Buddhists who have escaped the cycle of karma through Jesus Christ. If you or someone you know have been set free through reading this book, we would love to hear from you!
Please send your testimony via this link:
www.discover.org.au/contact/testimonies

We pray you share the Good News to many open-hearted Buddhists who are searching for a lasting answer to suffering. To contact our ministry, email:
info@discover.org.au